AF810078

Sister, Own Your Finances

Financial Blueprint to Become Your Own Financial Hero

This book is not intended to provide personalized legal, accounting, financial or investment advice. Readers are encouraged to seek the counsel of competent professionals with regard to such matters. This book is intended to provide accurate information in regards to the financial subject matter covered. Nonetheless, inadvertent errors can occur, and financial products, market conditions, rules and regulations, and laws or interpretations of laws are subject to change. Consequently, the publisher and the author specifically disclaim any liability, loss, or risk that may be incurred as a consequence of the use and applications, directly or indirectly, of any information presented in this book. Because every reader's financial situation and goals are unique, it is recommended that a financial, legal or tax professional be consulted prior to implementing any of the suggestions herein.

Copyright © 2022 by **Elizabeth Rose** All rights reserved Published by beyondthebookmedia.com All rights reserved. No part of this publication may be reproduced, distributed, or transmitted in any form or by any means, including photocopying, recording, or other electronic or mechanical methods, without the prior written permission of the publisher, except in the case of brief quotations embodied in critical reviews and certain other noncommercial uses permitted by copyright law. For permission requests, write to the publisher, addressed "Attention: Permissions Coordinator," at the address below. Limit of Liability/Disclaimer of Warranty: While the publisher and author have used their best efforts in preparing this book, they make no representations of warranties with respect to the accuracy or completeness of the contents of this book and specifically disclaim any implied warranties or merchantability or fitness for a particular purpose. No warranty may be created or extended by sales representatives or written sales materials. The advice and strategies contained herein may not be suitable for your situation. You should consult with a professional where appropriate. Neither the publisher nor author shall be liable for damages arising here from. Beyond The Book Media, LLC Alpharetta. GA www.beyondthebookmedia.com The publisher is not responsible for websites that are not owned by the publisher. **ISBN –978-1-953788-65-8 (Printed)**

Sister, Own Your Finances

Financial Blueprint to Become Your Own Financial Hero

Elizabeth Rose

Dedication:

This book is dedicated to my daughters, Christen and Amanda. From the time they were little, they have inspired me to reach for the stars. I yearned for them to have a well-rounded and prosperous life. And in that process, it motivated me to become a better person and a better mom. I am so proud and grateful for the beautifully strong women and mothers they have become. They have blessed me with five incredible grandkids who they are shaping into amazing young people. And above all, I am grateful to God, my Father, for walking beside me and lighting my path.

Table of Contents

Preface

As a single mom of two little girls, I recall what it feels like to be alone, broke, and lost. To not have a clue how to make ends meet, much less get ahead. To live paycheck to paycheck with a scarcity mindset, wondering how I would provide for my kids.

The father of my girls, my first husband, and I were high school sweethearts. We married during college and divorced after seven years of marriage. We grew in different directions. It's not so much that we grew apart as we grew into who we were each created to be. And those two people were not a match.

Life improved for my girls when I got a better job with a much higher income. Looking back, I was so thrilled to land this job, yet I felt it was a bit over my head. But that was insecurity talking. I remember feeling scared to death, and I thought they had made a mistake in hiring me. I felt I wasn't qualified. But I was. I was fully capable of the responsibilities that came with this position.

And then life turned another unexpected corner. I married my boss. This life change expanded the world for my daughters and me. I became friends with professional athletes, recording artists, songwriters, and other celebrities. I came to know many people in government offices across the U.S. and had an incredible friend group. This opened my eyes to a much larger world. Not only were great relationships formed, but I also actively participated in some major charity events that supported causes that touched my heart.

Sound like a white picket fence? Don't believe those dreamy ideals. There was a price for all of that. Although I didn't realize it initially, I gave up myself, independence, and self-confidence for that life.

Every decision in life, every encounter, and every relationship can alter or influence your life. What is most important is what you choose to do with it. Do you take the good, the best, and tuck it in your heart and treasure it? Allow the good to help you grow to your next level? Or do you take the disappointments, the deceptions, the hate spilled into anger and arguments and hold on to them?

It's all about the perspective you choose. You can choose to be a victim or let the testing refine you. Did you know diamonds are carbon crystals that form deep within the Earth (in the dark, in hiding) under incredibly high temperatures and extreme pressure (stress)? Oh, how I hope you choose to be a diamond!

My second divorce was a financial wrecking ball. In the end, he was awarded our homes, and I got a vacant lot in another country. That almost sounds like lyrics to a country song. I got to keep my car. That was good!

I hadn't worked full-time in years because he wanted me available for occasional business trips with him. But really, I think it was just his ego. As a result, I had no money of my own and no access to our marital money. Plus, I had lost years of professional development.

The divorce was long and nasty. I had a choice. I could let it destroy me, or I could choose to stand up and fight for my dignity, my strength, and my spirit. I chose to fight for myself. I resumed my career. I focused. I leaned in. I pressed on to discover my identity and create a life of purpose.

It wasn't easy. I promise you I've had to fight voices in my head that say I'm not enough. I don't measure up. I'm not good enough. I'm too old. I'm not smart enough. Don't believe the enemy.

Which person will you be? The victim or the beneficiary? We have both of these personalities within us. Think about Simon Peter. He was Simon until Jesus gave him the name Peter. Some days he acted like Simon, and other days he stepped into Peter. Jesus sifted him to bring out the best in him. Whatever season of life you are in, allow God to sift you and mold you. Take back the power He has given you and step into who He has created you to be.

And remember this: becoming the person we are created to be is a process, a journey with many pit stops, hills and valleys, rest areas, detours, and roadblocks. Stay the course. He is with you.

Acknowledgments

Thank you to the many clients who sat across the table from me and trusted me with your hurt, anger, and fear. I have been honored to hear your stories and provide solutions to help you begin the next chapter of your lives.

A special thanks to Bill Hart, my first business coach and the first person I spoke to about my desire to be a lighthouse for women who have found themselves suddenly single. Your support and encouragement helped me get started.

Without the input of Nick Thomas, I may never have thought of writing a book on this topic. Thank you, Nick.

A huge thank you to Jody Bruns, founder of Divorce Lending Association. Thank you for being a pioneer and champion in this important aspect of finance. You have paved the way in our industry, bringing awareness, perspective, and ongoing education greatly needed and appreciated.

Thank you, Rene Rodriquez, for your friendship. You helped me regain clarity and reminded me of who I am. You, and the work you do, inspire me to embrace all I was created to be in this life.

Thank you, Jayme Dixson, my Bible teacher and spiritual girlfriend, for speaking life into me and prophesying that God has equipped me to be a blessing. I love you, my friend.

To my mother, who told me when I was barely a teenager that I could be and do anything I wanted in life, and to my father, who instilled in me a strong work ethic, thank you for believing in me, encouraging me, and supporting me in all phases of life.

Mostly, I thank God for His divine inspiration.

Introduction

Finding yourself suddenly single is one of the most difficult life changes to experience. It can be emotional, expensive, and destructive. In short, it can be ugly and messy. And it often leaves each person off balance for some time as they cope with new routines, expectations, and demands.

As far as women have come since entering the workforce decades ago, many women have continued to delegate financial responsibilities and decisions to men. Once required to take on the responsibility, this has often led to overwhelming feelings of lack of knowledge, clarity, and confidence in taking hold of the financial decisions for themselves, their children, and their households.

Sadly, many women have taken on a victim mentality from these experiences of feeling overwhelmed. And I say to them, "You are not a victim!" Do not wear that badge. Perhaps you are being sifted as God refines you into the next phase of your life. But you are not a victim.

In this book, you will discover:

- How a healthy mindset and self-worth is vital to financial strength and stability

- The Basic Rules of Money and the power of compounding

- How to organize your assets and liabilities

- A way to map out your numbers to create a plan

- The difference between good debt and bad debt
- How debt and your credit are related
- The 3 snowballs in eliminating your debt
- How to begin building your net worth
- The various types of insurance to protect your loved ones and your assets
- Ways to divide the home in a divorce
- The value of home ownership

In addition to learning the lessons and information shared in this book, you'll also have access to worksheets to help you accomplish the methods outlined. Even if you divorce in peace, the stress of divorce is real and can't be erased. My mission and desire is to equip and empower women who are suddenly single to have successful outcomes so they can seize this opportunity to create their future on their terms – to become their own financial hero.

In short, I hope to help you avoid some of the mistakes other women and I have made during and immediately after divorce. I want to encourage, empower, and equip you to take control of your financial future. There is no better time to start than right now.

I believe no one should go through a divorce or any situation that finds you suddenly single and its aftermath alone. Don't let pride get in the way. Surround yourself with like-minded professionals – attorneys, financial planners, certified divorce financial planners, CPAs, divorce lenders, counselors, and mental health professionals – who are committed to working together as a team to help you have a successful outcome.

"By wisdom a house is built, and through understanding it is established; through knowledge its rooms are filled with rare and beautiful treasures." — Proverbs 24:3-4

Chapter 1

Straighten Your Crown

"Hold on, don't let go. Just take one step closer, one foot in front of the other, you'll get through this. Just follow the light in the darkness. You're gonna be okay." —from You're Gonna Be Ok, written by Brian & Jenn Johnson

As we start this journey together, I pray those words come to life for you. Hold on. Put one foot in front of the other. Follow the light. With every step, you're getting closer to being okay. Closer to being rock solid good!

Our mindset is so important, especially when it comes to money. And before we can deal with money, we must get our minds right and remember our identity - who we are - and deal with our hearts, thoughts, and minds.

Philippians 4:8 says, "Whatever is true, whatever is noble, whatever is right, whatever is pure, whatever is lovely, whatever is admirable—if anything is excellent or praiseworthy—think about such things." The Message version puts it like this: "Summing it all up, friends, I'd say you'll do best by filling your minds and meditating on things true, noble, reputable, authentic, compelling, gracious—the best, not the worst; the beautiful, not the ugly; things to praise, not things to curse. Put into practice what you learned from me, what you heard and saw and realized. Do that, and God, who makes everything work together, will work you into his most excellent harmonies."

It's probably tough to think of a suddenly single life turning into a harmony, much less an excellent one. It is often hard to think about whatever is lovely, as Paul instructs us. Believe me, I know. But with God...anything is possible!

When I was going through my divorce, and for several months afterward, my mind was all over the place. Tears would come unexpectedly. Anger. Bitterness. Frustration. Confusion. Decisions seemed impossible to make. If that is where you are right now, that's okay. Take a deep breath, take a walk, and spend some time with God. Ask Him for help. Spend time working on your inner self to gain some calmness and peace.

If you feel like a hot mess right now, you won't forever. Just today, I was having lunch with some girlfriends who have experienced a divorce. One has been divorced for three years. She said she thought it was the end of the world at the time. She couldn't imagine ever finding happiness again. She shared that her family and friends encouraged her, telling her it would get better. She didn't believe them. And now, today at lunch, she is laughing as she tells this story. She finds it hard to imagine now that she had such little hope.

If only our future self could show up and pull us out of the mud puddle.

You Are Not Alone

There is a difference between being alone and the feeling of loneliness. Loneliness seems temporal, whereas aloneness seems longer lasting and perhaps even like a life sentence. And it's quite possible during this season, you feel alone.

When I went through my divorce, I had very few friends that could relate. Actually, I had none that could relate. My husband was a C-suite executive of a Fortune 100 company. None of my friends had that type of home life or financial life. There were client dinners, last-minute trips, big events, gala's, charity functions, entertainment, and plenty of pressure. Of course, all my friends thought we had the "white-picket-fence" life. Behind the front door of our beautiful home, things were not so "white-picket-fence." Life was messy.

My husband had just gone through a massive corporate merger when our marriage fell apart. His world had been shaken for months, the demands on him had changed, and he lost some of his autonomy in running the company. He seemed to have lost his identity. He had driven a wedge between my daughters and me (he was their stepdad), which caused me great pain, and I'm sure it did my girls as well. Needless to say, there was plenty of stress building in the household. Then one day, he walked out, just days after Thanksgiving. I didn't see it coming.

A year or so earlier, I returned to work after taking a break to spend time at home with my daughters. I was ready to get out of the house, restart my career, and be challenged. Plus, I wanted to have something to do. Thank goodness I had done so. With my husband walking out, I needed something to throw myself into. And because my daughters were now teenagers, they were busy with their lives and really didn't want to hang out with mom.

My husband and I remained separated for over two years. Following the merger, he moved to our second home in Mexico. Talk about living in separate residences! I remained in the States and continued to work and raise my daughters. We were the classic definition of estranged. We were only connected by a piece of paper — our marriage license.

It was an odd couple of years. Truth be told, it was a hard, heartbreaking, and lonely couple of years. I was legally married but had no husband. My girls were always on the go, doing what healthy teenagers do. And I was alone. Always alone.

I felt abandoned in every single way. All the day-to-day decisions were left to me. If anything broke in the house, I had to deal with it. If the kids challenged me like teenagers often do, I had no one to back me up. I had no access to money. Each month I had to give him the total of all the bills, and he would send money to cover them. Just enough. I realize to some women, that would be a blessing. And it was a blessing to me to have the overhead taken care of. Yet, it was a reminder that we never did have the union I longed for.

And the questions! From everyone. When is he coming back to the States? Why is he not living here? How do y'all manage living in different countries? When will you see him again? What about the girls? The questions were never-ending, and I felt like a failure. I had no answers.

Over two years later, my husband returned to the States, and we cohabitated for a few months. Then I asked to proceed with the divorce he had wanted, which I had been so against. We were strangers, and there was just no way to repair the damage.

At the time of our divorce, my oldest daughter, who was now 20, had decided to move back to our home state of Georgia. And my youngest daughter, age 18, was leaving for her first year of college.

My household of four (well, really, it had just been the three of us the last few years) quickly became a house of one. Me. Alone. Really alone. So I do know the feeling, and it is rotten, at least until you learn how to embrace it. Sister, I can't say that I did it well. Not even close. I didn't have a local support system. All of my family and friends were in Georgia. I had made some acquaintances in Texas but no real friends. We had not been living in Texas very long.

Without connections or resources to help me get through the difficult time, I did the only thing I could think of. I threw myself into work. I started my company.

I'll never forget a client of mine, a highly regarded financial advisor, telling me that I was going through three major life events all at one time: divorce, empty nesting, and starting a company. He cautioned me with gentleness. He also admired my strength. I didn't change a thing, yet it was so heartwarming that he would notice and talk with me about all that was going on in my life.

Starting a company was good medicine. It kept me busy by day and focused on something productive. Otherwise, I would have been in a puddle of tears every day. But nightfall always comes. I had too many nights of skipping dinner, working late, and drinking too much wine, all so I could collapse in bed and sleep through the feelings of being alone.

Where was this great God of ours? He was there. But I was so consumed with myself, fear, and grief (all those feelings that are not from God) that I didn't even reach out to Him for a while. Oh, I asked my women's bible group to pray for me. And I prayed too. But they were such brief prayers, the ones I call whisper or breath prayers because they are said almost under the breath. "God help me." "God, I can't do this." "God, this hurts so bad." "God, how am I supposed to do this?" But not once did I wait to hear from Him.

When I wasn't working, I felt like I was drifting through life. It is a hard place to live, and we don't have to. No matter how alone we think or feel we are, we aren't. Christ promises us He is with us. And He hears even those brief "breath" prayers. He is the El Roi, the God who sees, and Jehovah Shammah, the God who is there. When we quiet our minds and surrender to Him, we will find and feel His presence.

"The light shines in the darkness; and the darkness has not overcome it!" John 1:5

Thankfully, the light comes with each new day.

Beauty for Ashes

Some women embrace being single. For many others, becoming single again is painful. Following a divorce or the death of a spouse (and the aftermath) brings plenty of tears. I don't want to minimize the pain. It is real, and it is hard. So if you've just finished a good cry, dry your eyes and put your makeup on! We have work to do getting the financial house in order!

A large part of the work is rediscovering who we are; it is so vital. Our identity is the way we see ourselves, think about ourselves, how we are viewed by others and the world, and the characteristics that define us. Our identity is important to our health and wellbeing.

You may be wondering, what does this have to do with my money? Research shows there's a powerful connection between self-worth and net worth. Self-worth is defined as self-esteem. And self-esteem is defined as believing in one's own ability. Confidence in one's own worth.

Net worth is the amount by which your assets (what you own) exceed your liabilities (what you owe). If your assets exceed your liabilities, you have a positive net worth. Your net worth provides a snapshot of your financial situation at a specific moment in time.

Once examined, it's easy to see the connection. If self-esteem is believing in one's own worth, then our financial worth would reflect our belief. While no one should judge themself as a person by financial success, failure, or shortcomings, many people do. And sometimes, it isn't even consciously. The things we think and tell ourselves have an incredible ability to write themselves in our subconscious minds. Our behavior is directed primarily by our subconscious mind. Guard your thoughts!

And yes, money can impact whether someone has healthy self-esteem. What you believe about yourself affects pretty much everything in your life, including money. Have you ever known a beautiful woman who did not believe she was pretty? Or someone with a good physical build who only saw flaws? Or a mom who was doing a terrific job with her kids thinking she is lousy? Most of us believe incorrectly about ourselves. Our perspective of ourselves is skewed. We believe the labels society puts on us. In order to get a correct estimate of who we are, we must first understand who God says we are.

> Do you know what God says about you?

> Do you know how special you are?

You are a child of God Most High! That is something to certainly celebrate! A daughter of The King!

"But you are a chosen people, a royal priesthood, a holy nation, God's special possession, that you may declare the praises of him who called you out of darkness into his wonderful light;" 1 Peter 2:9

He made you.

"My frame was not hidden from you when I was being made in the secret place, when I was woven together in the depths of the earth." Psalm 139: 15

"I praise you because I am fearfully and wonderfully made." Psalm 139:14

He knew you before you were born.

"Your eyes saw my unformed body." Psalm 139:16

"For you created my inmost being; you knit me together in my mother's womb." Psalm 139:13

You are crowned.

"You have made them a little lower than the angels and crowned them with glory and honor." Psalm 8:5

You are created for a purpose.

"For we are his workmanship, created in Christ Jesus for good works, which God prepared beforehand, that we should walk in them." Ephesians 2:10 ESV

You are chosen.

"You did not choose Me, but I chose you, and appointed you that you might go and bear fruit – fruit that will last – and so that whatever you ask in my name the Father will give." John 15:16

You are a new creation.

"Therefore, if anyone is in Christ, the new creation has come. The old has gone; the new is here." 2 Corinthians 5:17

You are powerful, loved, and have a sound mind.

"For the Spirit God gave us does not make us timid, but gives us power, love, and self-discipline." 2 Timothy 1:7

You are strong.

"It is God who arms me with strength and keeps my way secure." Psalm 18:32

You are forgiven.

"I am writing to you, dear children, because your sins have been forgiving on account of his name." 1 John 2:12

You are forever loved.

"And I am convinced that nothing can ever separate us from God's love. Neither death nor life, neither angels nor demons, neither our fears for today nor our worries about tomorrow—not even the powers of hell can separate us from God's love." Romans 8:38 NLT

Oh, how He loves us! Agape love. Unconditional love. We are precious in His sight.

Have you ever stopped to consider that our Heavenly Father is the King of Kings, making you royalty? You are a beautiful daughter. Royalty. A princess of the Most High King. That, all by itself, should cause you to dry your eyes, put on your lipstick, stand up straight and behave like the princess you are!

You've got to remember that before you can take care of anyone or anything else-your kids, aging parents, your job, your finances, your household-you've got to take care of yourself.

Surround Yourself with Support

Finding a group of friends who will support and encourage you without the drama is very important. Without bashing your ex-husband. Without negative energy.

Be mindful of who you spend time with. For any of those friends who love to gossip, create drama, or have a touch of negativity, you need to put them on the back burner for this season. These types of people are not good for you right now. Surround yourself with encouragers. People who will build you up, not bring you down. People who won't "dog" your husband and stir the pot with drama. Those who will shine the light on you and lift you up. Those who will help you focus on moving forward, not staying stuck in the past.

In addition, it is time to surround yourself with some people who are good financial stewards. People who can give you wise counsel surrounding money and financial matters.

Remember the popular saying, "You are the equivalent of the five people you spend the most time with?" Think of the type of person you want those five people to be. Find them. Spend time with them. If you don't have the kinds of friends you want to be surrounded by, pray for God to bring them into your life. I've done that before, and He answered.

My women's bible study group was my salvation. The women in the group became my prayer partners and warriors. They have been an incredible blessing. I needed them to pray with me, check on me, invite me to lunch, and love on me. They gave me the kind of support that my other friends couldn't give.

You have His strength

You're stronger than you know. I realize you may not feel strong, or you are tired of being strong. Maybe you want someone else to be strong for you, for just a little while, so you can catch a breather. That is such a normal feeling. But you are going to have to find the strength.

So many times, I've had friends, family, and even acquaintances tell me I am strong. And so often, when I heard that, I wanted to throw a small temper tantrum for what was meant as a compliment. While I believe being strong is an asset, sometimes I don't want to have to be strong. I want someone else to do it. I want a break.

Much of the time, I didn't believe I was strong. I will never forget my husband saying to me, "You will fall on your face." When my husband spoke those words to me, he was calm, intimidating, and calculating. "You will fall on your face." And I believed him for a while. Those words haunted me for at least a year, perhaps longer.

At one point or another, most of us have a point in our life where we feel like we don't measure up. We aren't "good enough" by someone's definition, maybe even our own. Thankfully, when he said that to me, while I did halfway believe him, it made me mad. So I stood up tall and acted as strong as I could fake. I was totally faking it. There was no way I was going to let him see that he had gotten to me. I knew I had to fight the good fight. The fight that says:

...don't listen to the negative voices.

...you will not be destroyed.

...you can do this.

...you are strong.

...you WILL survive this.

It was a tough battle. His words, "You will fall on your face," were often much louder in my mind than the quiet inner voice that said, "I can do this."

Luckily, in time, my inner voice won. I remember reciting for months, "You can do all things through Christ." That was my mantra to maintain my strength. Focusing on this mantra re-wired my mind to think correctly. So, remember that in our weakness, He is made strong.

How do you find strength when you feel overwhelmed, stressed, tired, alone, and weak? It's different for everyone. One of the best things for me has been to pivot. To shift gears. I will do something totally different than what I am doing in the moments I begin to feel weak.

Here are a few suggestions:

- Take a walk.
- Put on some uplifting music.
- Play a musical instrument.
- Listen to a comedian or watch a funny movie and laugh aloud.
- Sing out loud, even if your singing is horrible.
- Get your nails done. Or your hair. Or your lashes. Whatever it is that you do to pamper yourself. Do that!
- Take a shower, wash your face, put on makeup, get out of your athletic clothes, and put on something pretty.
- Have lunch with a friend or two.
- Call your mother or grandmother.
- Take a cake or casserole to an elderly neighbor. It's okay if you purchased it pre-made.
- Clean out your closet or garage. Or go dig in the dirt in your flower garden. Sometimes an activity like that which takes energy gives you energy. Your mental focus is directed on the task, and you just might not think about all the other stuff that keeps you up at night and stresses you out.
- Schedule an appointment with a financial planner, a tax planner, a home organizer, a counselor, or someone you need assistance from to move the needle forward. Sounds a bit different, I know.

But often, accomplishing something as simple as making an appointment takes a load off your shoulders.

Find something to shift gears. Put on strength. It's your portion. God has instructed you to put on strength.

"She is clothed with strength and dignity, she can laugh at the days to come." Proverbs 31:25

Put on strength and dignity just like you slip into your favorite jeans and tee.

The King James version says, "Strength and honor are her clothing; and she shall rejoice in time to come."

Imagine that. Our clothing is strength and honor!

Look at the Amplified Bible version. "Strength and dignity are her clothing and her position is strong and secure; And she smiles at the future [knowing that she and her family are prepared]."

The Passion translation says, "Bold power and glorious majesty are wrapped around her as she laughs with joy over the latter days."

When exploring this in the Blue Letter Bible[1] , I learned that strength in the Hebrew means strength, strong, power, might, boldness, loud, and mighty. It further explains strength in various applications: force, security, majesty, and praise.

I can't begin to count the number of times I have recited that verse in my mind as I felt hurt, disappointed, or insignificant. It strengthens me in ways hard to describe.

Here's what the dictionary has to say about strength and dignity.

Noun **streŋ(k)th**[2]

- the quality or state of being strong; bodily or muscular power.
- mental power, force, or vigor.
- moral power, firmness, or courage.
- power by reason of influence, authority, resources, numbers, etc.

Noun, **plural dig•ni•tee**[3]

- bearing, conduct, or speech indicative of self-respect or appreciation of the formality or gravity of an occasion or situation.
- nobility or elevation of character; worthiness: dignity of sentiments.
- relative standing; rank.
- a sign or token of respect: an impertinent question unworthy of the dignity of an answer.

Do you see the many references to royalty? Nobility. Elevated rank or character.

Dignity says, "I am composed. I am worthy. I have self-respect." Dignity is lovely.

The next time you are feeling in the dumps, try reciting this verse and remind yourself who you are and whose you are!

As we prepare ourselves for the business of starting fresh and getting our financial house in order, let's not forget to put on the full armor of God as well.

"Therefore, put on the full armor of God, so that when the day of evil comes, you may be able to stand your ground, and after you have done everything, to stand. 14 Stand firm then, with the belt of truth buckled around your waist, with the breastplate of righteousness in place, 15 and with your feet fitted with the readiness that comes from the gospel of peace. 16 In addition to all this, take up the shield of faith, with which you can extinguish all the flaming arrows of the evil one. 17 Take the helmet of salvation and the sword of the Spirit, which is the word of God." Ephesians 6:10-17

Stand up tall. Now it is time to act like the amazing woman God created you to be. It's time to straighten your crown. Own it!

Chapter 2

Possess the Basics

When I was growing up, people didn't talk about money, at least not in my little world. And even in my home, I rarely heard my parents discuss money. Now, that's not to say that I didn't frequently hear the "Do you think money grows on trees?" comment! In fact, I heard a lot of these types of phrases. I was raised to believe that there was just enough, but not more than enough.

In my early 20s, I recall my mother telling me that she never knew what my dad's paycheck looked like until she took a job at the bank. And I don't mean "looked like" as in the amount. I mean the color, the logo, etc. She had never seen one. Then, when she was working at the bank, she had many customers who worked for this employer and saw a payroll check for the first time. My father wasn't being secretive, and my mom didn't have her head in the sand. It's just the way things were back then.

If you grew up in the '60s or '70s, you might have a similar story. That's just the way things were. Money, among other things, was considered a private and personal matter. No one used their outside voice when talking about money.

It's interesting to think about the money perceptions of a twelve-year-old girl in the early '70s. I thought my cousin was rich because she went to a private school. She lived in the same neighborhood. Her parents worked their fannies off to afford the private school. They were just as middle class as us. The only difference was her mom worked a full-time job, and my mom worked from time to time.

Society has changed since those days. People aren't as quiet or private about their finances as they once were.

Yet, the majority of people still have major issues around money. I attribute this to the lack of financial education in our schools. You don't know what you don't know.

In my second marriage, my husband was a C-Suite executive. He was very giving in many ways, but he was a narcissist and loved to control. One of the ways he did this was through money. We did not have a joint checking account. As a result, I had no access to money. I had to ask for it. I even had to ask for grocery money and money to run the house. I didn't have any of my own money because he had urged me to stop working so I could live a life of luxury (ha!) and travel with him on occasion. Let me tell you, there is nothing luxurious about having to ask someone for money for every single little thing. That life of luxury looked just like a white picket fence on the outside, but inside the walls of the fancy home lived a woman (me) who was broke.

Having money doesn't necessarily equal having success. Money does not equal prosperity. Many people appear to have a perfect life and plenty of material wealth. Don't let the highlight reel on social media fool you. Many people with wealth live with broken hearts. Or are unfulfilled. Many with material wealth are living paycheck to paycheck. Looks are deceiving at times.

People relate to money in different ways. Some people have a healthy perspective on money. Others have been shaped by all sorts of ideas of money being evil, immoral, and a societal evil. And some people are just complacent about it.

What does the Bible *really* say about money?

"But remember the LORD your God, for it is he who gives you the ability to produce wealth, and so confirms his covenant, which he swore to your ancestors, as it is today." Deuteronomy 8:18

"Dishonest money dwindles away, but whoever gathers money little by little makes it grow." Proverbs 13:11

"The plans of the diligent lead to profit as surely as haste leads to poverty." Proverbs 21:5

"Four things on earth are small, yet they are extremely wise: Ants are creatures of little strength, yet they store up their food in the summer." Proverbs 30:24-25 (This sounds like it is all about ants and storing food, but it is wisdom on gathering and saving.)

"And it is a good thing to receive wealth from God and the good health to enjoy it. To enjoy your work and accept your lot in life—this is indeed a gift from God." Ecclesiastes 5:19[4]

"I am the Lord Your God, who brought you up out of Egypt. Open wide your mouth and I will fill it." Psalms 81:10

Many people believe money is evil and rich people are wicked. But the love of money is the root of all evil. Not money itself. Wealth doesn't make a person good or bad. An individual is good or bad before they ever get wealthy. Your beliefs about money dictate your relationship with it. If one believes that money is the root of all evil, then he will most likely have a poor relationship with money.

Rules of Money

"Money is only a tool. It will take you wherever you wish, but it will not replace you as the driver."

~ Ayn Rand[5]

Money isn't good or bad. Money is simply a means of exchange, a form of payment that is generally accepted.

"Money never sleeps." We've all probably heard that expression but may wonder what it means. It means that money is always in motion. In fact, our Federal Reserve is always looking at the velocity of money (how quickly it moves) to ensure our economy is moving at a healthy pace.

Money changes hands. It changes forms. You get paid from your job, then you take that money and pay for your house, car, and utilities, run through a drive-through, stop at the grocery store, etc. And every one of those places takes your money and uses it to buy more products, pay employees, etc. And those employees go on to do the same thing you are doing. And those merchants you bought the products from have bills they pay and employees too.

Money never stands still. The speed at which money moves from the employer to you, to the marketplace to pay for goods and services, then from the retailer to the manufacturer or producer, and so on, is called the velocity of money. The velocity of money (fast or slow) is an indication of inflation or lack thereof.

Simply put, money facilitates exchanges in the economy. The individual chooses how to obtain it, keep it, save it, and exchange it. Currency doesn't care what a person does with it; it is not emotional like some of us.

Here's the important thing to remember: either you control your money, or it controls you. Money doesn't care if it is spent or saved. It doesn't care if it is loaned out or borrowed. In order to control money, it must be managed, which means you must pay attention to it.

Here are some foundational rules regarding finances:

The first rule of financial freedom: Pay attention to your money!

If money is constantly moving, we need to be on the offense to tell it where to go. Managing money is all about action. WE must pay attention to our money and learn to tell our money what to do (action). Otherwise, it will manage us.

Some of us have done an amazing job managing our money. We have figured out the formula. However, that is the minority. Most Americans don't adhere to this first rule. Why? Because we don't know what we don't know. We were never taught. The school system in America doesn't teach financial literacy in most states. For many of us, our parents didn't really know much either–they just did the best they could. And they may have been figuring it out as they went.

Furthermore, we are a nation of consumers. We live in a society of keeping up with the Joneses. We want a thing, and we want it now. Immediate gratification. And if we don't have the money to buy it, we have plastic.

Here are some terrible statistics that illustrate what this lack of education has done:

- Approximately 80% of Americans are in debt[6]

- Over 70% live paycheck to paycheck[7]

- 69% have less than 1,000 in savings – not even enough if the hot water heater goes out[8]

- 45% ages 45 – 54 have NO retirement savings[9]

- 53% ages 45- 65+ have less than $10K in retirement savings[10]

- 56% lose sleep over money concerns[11]

In 2020, banks charged over $12.4 billion in overdraft fees[12], which tells us that too many of us don't pay attention to or know how to budget money. It also begs the question, do people balance their checking account anymore?

<u>The second rule of money: Get your mindset in gear</u>

What we think matters–a lot!

In the parable of the Sower in Matthew 13:3-8, it tells us:

"a farmer went out to sow his seed. As he was scattering the seed, some fell along the path, and the birds came and ate it up. Some fell on rocky places, where it did not have much soil. It sprang up quickly because the soil was shallow. But when the sun came up, the plants were scorched, and they withered because they had no root. Other seed fell among thorns, which grew up and choked the plants. Still, other seed fell on good soil, where it produced a crop – a hundred, sixty or thirty times what was sown."

It's important that you prepare your mindset (soil) so that as you learn these concepts and create and work your plan, you will adopt a new way of thinking about your money. This will ensure you get long-lasting results. The harvest. The reward. A life free of financial worry.

Your money mindset is the subconscious feelings and thoughts you have developed about money. These are the result of life experiences that have been imprinted in your subconscious over time. Just like our mind controls our brain, it controls our actions, whether wanted or not. A poor or negative money mindset can keep you from financial health and bring anxiety and stress. Anxiety and stress are toxic to the brain. But the good news is your money mindset can be shifted to more positive money thoughts!

Beliefs are not necessarily true, yet we think they are. A belief is an assumed truth. A belief is an idea or principle that we judge to be true. A belief is often something we have convinced ourselves is true. Beliefs can be changed.

At one time, people believed the earth was flat. They believed it to be true. But is the earth flat? Heck no! Remember the Wright brothers? Even after they built the first controlled flight of a power-driven airplane, people still did not believe in them or their idea of flight. But it was already true.

Our mind is comprised of three levels of awareness: the conscious, the preconscious, and the unconscious (also referred to as subconscious) minds. Referring to it as the unconscious mind helps highlight its powerful influence.

The conscious mind contains all the thoughts, desires, memories, and feelings people are aware of at any given point in time. The keyword is aware.

The preconscious mind is anything that can be brought forward (recall) into the conscious mind. For instance, you might not be thinking of your phone number, but you can easily recall it if someone asks.

The unconscious mind is extraordinary and incredibly powerful. It works 24 hours a day running the body - breathing, pumping blood, keeping your organs functioning, and so on. It does its job without instruction. The unconscious mind is recording everything, Whether awake or asleep. And it is the unconscious mind that is calling most of the shots. It is the primary source of all human behavior.

Here's an example. When you first learned to ride a bike, your conscious mind was engaged in the process. Once you finally mastered riding, your unconscious mind took over. All the automatic movements are guided by the unconscious mind. You don't have to think about how to ride a bike; you just hop on and ride.

See how powerful the unconscious mind is! And it has been recording every experience, conversation, skill, thought, belief, and so much more. The unconscious mind does not discern truth from fiction, which means it is storing many things that are not true.

Thoughts run around in our subconscious minds without notice, mostly because we do not pay attention to the thoughts that created the belief. At some point, these thoughts are accepted as truth and become our beliefs. Over time, they become a reality. And then, they reign over our minds. We must find those hijackers and find out what they are made of.

To uncover beliefs about money, contemplate these questions:

- What does money mean to me?
- Do I consistently worry about money?
- Do I believe I'll never have enough money?
- Do I believe I deserve to be financially comfortable or even wealthy?

While you may think you know your attitude toward money, it's possible that you are not fully aware of how your unconscious feels towards money. This is important to understand because it shapes your decision-making. You may not be fully aware of your unconscious thoughts about money because most of us are not even aware of our conscious thoughts.

Capturing rogue thoughts is one of the first steps in mindfulness and monitoring thoughts before being recorded in the unconscious. To do this, observe every thought. I know that sounds challenging. Try to pay attention. As Paul writes, "We demolish arguments and every pretension that sets itself up against the knowledge of God, and we take captive every thought to make it obedient to Christ." 2 Corinthians 10:5

Take captive every thought. Ask yourself, "Is it true?" This helps to stop the negative impact in its tracks.

Here's a great challenge to get started with: start each day instructing yourself to pay attention to what you are thinking. Throughout the day, stop and ask yourself if you have been paying attention to your thinking. Then think about the thoughts that have come up. Examine them. Explore them. Over time, you will tune into your thought life more naturally and will be able to easily stop yourself from going down a rabbit hole of negative thoughts.

One of my favorite scripture verses regarding thought-life is found in the letter from Paul to the Philippians. "...whatever is true, whatever is noble, whatever is right, whatever is pure, whatever is lovely, whatever is admirable–if anything is excellent or praiseworthy–think about such things." Philippians 4:8

The third rule of money: Create a plan

Many women I have worked with tell me that they felt incredibly overwhelmed with finances once they were on their own again. Feelings of being overwhelmed generally come when a lack of control is present.

The purpose of a plan is to help you stay organized and on track so that you meet your financial obligations and save and invest, building that nest egg. Having a plan gives us a sense of control. Creating a budget will also help either get out of debt or stay out of debt.

The budget provides the roadmap for achieving your goals. It will help achieve savings goals, emergency planning goals, retirement goals, etc.

Some people think of a budget like a diet–it deprives us of those things we enjoy most. It does not have to be that way. A budget can include some of your special treats. It also helps you see how much is wasted on things that perhaps aren't that important. If getting your nails done is important, then, by all means, put that on your budget. If you want to have a weekly night out on the town with friends or your kids, budget that too. It's okay to spend money. It's okay to treat yourself or buy things you like. Just make it part of your plan. The bottom line is that it is important to know where and how much is being spent.

The fourth rule of money: Prioritize Tithing, Saving, Investing

This seems to be the most difficult shift for people and yet a very important financial concept. Tithing followed by saving are concepts that seem to get swept under the rug too frequently. Everyone works hard for a paycheck. Hard! And then quickly spend it on the mortgage, utilities, creditors, etc. And while it is important to pay bills on time, why are we so willing to put everything in front of God? And in front of personal savings and our future?

Tithing and saving first is a proven money habit that can boost wealth. Set aside a certain portion of income every pay period.

Once the amount is determined, commit to the plan, and put it in the spending blueprint we will discuss in the coming chapters. When payroll is by direct deposit, the easiest way to create this habit is to set up the direct deposit to go into the checking account with a portion into a savings account. With the tithe, set it up on automatic draft to hit on payday. That way, the money usually isn't missed. Plus, it helps build the muscle in being consistent.

"Do not save what is left after spending, but spend what is left after saving."
~ Warren Buffet[13]

Zero-Sum Game

After everything is calculated (income, tithe, savings, and expenses), hopefully, there will be money left over. Most of us will spend that money. Instead, take those remaining dollars and move them elsewhere, leaving the account at zero. First, use the remaining dollars to apply toward credit card debt. When paying extra towards debt, you save interest expenses over the long term. Eventually, when debt is paid to zero, those monthly funds can now be added to savings or the investments bucket. After moving those leftover dollars to debt or savings, the total will be zero. Hence, zero-sum game!

Why should it be drawn down to zero? It will disappear if the money isn't removed from the household into a savings or investment vehicle! Take my word. I used to be an expert spender. It will get spent. We subconsciously think of it as available and discretionary and spend it.

The fifth rule of money: Create an emergency fund

Everyone needs a fund to cover unexpected expenses when life happens. Sadly, the majority of Americans don't have $1,000 in savings. Whether a hot water heater bursts, a tire blows, or the refrigerator dies, it is critical to have a fund to cover these expenses. Otherwise, we tend to pull out the plastic and rack up more debt. Of course, this defeats the purpose of becoming debt-free!

An emergency fund should be at least $1,000 to around $2500. These funds should be handy and kept in a regular savings account.

The emergency fund is not for big purchases. It is for emergencies. It's for the hot water heater that bursts. Or the tire blow-out. This money must not be spent unless it fits an emergency label. In advance, make a list of situations that would be labeled emergency.

If moving a lump sum into a special savings account just for emergencies is out of reach, start saving. Starting small is fine. Set up a recurring transfer of $10, $25, $50, or whatever is achievable regularly to go into the emergency fund savings account each pay period.

Start somewhere, even if it is starting small. Just start.

This emergency savings account must not be attached to a primary checking account for overdraft protection. Why not? Because we are human. Knowing it is there will lead to swiping that dangerous debit card. Then, panic sets in because the money has dwindled without you realizing it. It is easier to just say no. Just don't do it.

Setting aside some money helps us build our financial muscles. It may also give us a feeling of reward, creating much-needed excitement, encouragement, or motivation to keep going.

The sixth rule of money: Educate thyself

With all my heart, I believe that no matter your age, education level, career status, or situation, you are more than capable of taking charge of your financial house and securing your future and becoming your own financial hero. All you need is a roadmap, some tools, and sound financial knowledge. And this journey all starts with taking the first step, which you've already done.

Many women have relied on men to take care of the financial planning and take care of them, perhaps, to some degree. While I taught my daughters not to put their financial stability and future in someone else's hands, this wisdom didn't come until after my divorce. It is important to be responsible for one's own finances, whether married or single.

For some reason, women have been led to believe that men are better at money and financial matters. Yet, if men were doing such a great job of taking care of their family's financial future, why do 55% of Americans aged 45-50 have no savings? My guess is that men aren't any better than women. And women can be just as good as men.

Owning the responsibility for your finances is critical. It may sound contrarian; however, women actually need more financial planning than men. There are many reasons for this. First, women live longer than men. Women live 5.7 years longer, according to actuaries in the insurance industry. Women are also active longer than men. What this means is women need to plan for a longer and more active life, which will require money.

Money Concepts

"An investment in knowledge pays the best interest." – Benjamin Franklin

The concepts in this chapter form the foundation for understanding money. The more you understand, the more equipped you will be to handle whatever comes your way. And hopefully, you will be inspired to stash some cash and build your net worth.

Compounding Interest

Compounding is the ability of an asset to generate earnings, which are then reinvested to generate their own earnings. In other words, compounding refers to generating earnings from previous earnings. To break it down further, it is earning interest off interest.

In order for this to work, it requires two things: 1) the reinvestment of earnings and 2) time. The more time you give your investments, the more you can accelerate the income potential of your original investment.

Let's say $10,000 is invested into purchasing McDonald's stock. The first year, pretend the share value rises 20%. Your investment is now worth $12,000.

Since it is doing so well, you decide to hold the stock. In Year 2, the shares appreciate (go up) another 20%. As a result, the $12,000 grows to $14,400.

In the first year, the shares appreciated 20%, or $2,000. In the second year, the 20% is $2,400, so more dollars than last year. This is because the $2,000 you gained in the first year grew by 20%. You earned off your initial principal of $10,000 plus the $2,000 growth from the first year.

Extend out 25 years to see what those earnings can do...

That same $10,000 invested at 20% annually (with reinvesting the interest) would grow to almost $1,000,000 over 25 years without you adding any extra money.

This math can be fun!

Now, I am not suggesting investments will produce 20% growth. They probably won't. I am simply trying to get your attention on the value of compounding. The value is in reinvesting your interest, the growth rate, and time. Time cannot be ignored.

Albert Einstein called compound interest "the greatest mathematical discovery of all time." Why might he have called it that? Perhaps because it can be applied by everyday people to everyday life. This greatest discovery of compounding has the ability to transform your money into a highly powerful income-generating tool.

To demonstrate, let's look at another example, a conservative one: If you invest $10,000 today at 6%, it will grow to $10,600 in one year ($10,000 x 1.06). Now let's say that the $600 gain from interest is left in the account for another year. Your balance is $10,600. If you continue to earn the same rate of 6%, your investment will grow to $11,236.00 ($10,600 x 1.06) by the end of the second year. Because you reinvested that $600, it works together with the original investment, earning you $636 in the second year.

In the third year, you do the same. You keep all the interest in the account, and now it is earning interest. Assuming you earn the same 6% rate, your investment grows to $11,910 by the end of the third year.

Here's the mathematical process:

$10,000 x 1.06 = $10,600 (you earned $600 in interest)

$10,600 x 1.06 = $11,236 (you earned $636 in interest)

$11,236 x 1.06 = $11,910 (you earned $674 in interest)

You just picked up $1,236 in two years without doing anything. You might think that is chump change and may not get too excited or motivated by it. But I bet if I rang your doorbell two years from now and offered you a check for $1,236, you would be pleasantly surprised and gladly take the check. Am I right, or am I right?

For compounding to work, it requires two things. First, the reinvestment of your earnings, the interest. And secondly, time. The sooner you start, the longer the time horizon, the more money you will end up with.

Penny Story

My granddaughter loved the game "Would You Rather?" and she would always come up with the strangest scenarios, such as "Would you rather be eaten by an alligator or a shark?" My answer is neither!

So, here's a "Would You Rather?" question for you: Would you rather have 1 million dollars or a penny doubled for 30 days?

Before reading any further, stop and contemplate that question. Which would you rather?

If you did the math, you discovered that the magical penny is the correct answer, and by a long shot.

By choosing the penny doubled every day for 30 days, at the end of a month, you'd have $10,737,418.24. Quite a bit more than $1,000,000[14].

Here's the chart of a Penny Doubled-

Day 1: $0.01	Day 11: $10.24	Day 21: $10,485.76
Day 2: $0.02	Day 12: $20.48	Day 22: $20,971.52
Day 3: $0.04	Day 13: $40.96	Day 23: $41,943.04
Day 4: $0.08	Day 14: $81.92	Day 24: $83,886.08
Day 5: $0.16	Day 15: $163.84	Day 25: $167,772.16
Day 6: $0.32	Day 16: $327.68	Day 26: $335,544.32
Day 7: $0.64	Day 17: $655.36	Day 27: $671,088.64
Day 8: $1.28	Day 18: $1,310.72	Day 28: $1,342,177.28
Day 9: $2.56	Day 19: $2,621.44	Day 29: $2,684,354.56
Day 10: $5.12	Day 20: $5,242.88	Day 30: $5,368,709.12

This is the power of compounding, ladies!

Compound interest is the holy grail of saving. But in the early years, it can be about as exciting as watching grass grow or paint dry. Some say Einstein called compound interest the 8th Wonder of the World. After looking at this chart above, you may agree it is a wonder of sorts.

Rule of 72

The number 72 is not just any old number or age. There is a very important money formula around the number 72 called the "Rule of 72"[15]. And it is all about doubling your money. It's a good rule to know!

This formula says that to find the number of years required to double your money at a given interest rate, you just divide the interest rate into 72. For example, if you want to know how long it will take to double your money at eight percent interest, divide 8 into 72, and the answer is 9 years to double your money.

You can also apply the formula using the years as the focal point. If I want my money to double in 6 years, I divide 72 by 6. The result is I need to earn 12% on my money in order for my money to double.

Simple as that!

Understanding the Rule of 72 helps you see how interest can help accelerate your savings. It also demonstrates the value of time and starting early.

Build your Financial Muscle

Consider the parable about planting a tree. When is the best time to plant a tree? 25 years ago. The next best time is today. Today is a good day to learn personal finance and put a plan together.

Giving ourselves the gift of financial education is one of the wisest things we can do. Of course, seeking advice from financial professionals is smart, yet it is also wise to do your own investigation and research.

As far as self-education, you may be wondering where to start, what to read, and so forth. Read financial periodicals, books, blogs, and articles written by well-regarded financial authors. Read often. Never stop learning.

Here are a few suggestions of great books to get you started:

Rich Dad Poor Dad–Robert Kiyosaki

Think and Grow Rich–Napoleon Hill

The Millionaire Next Door–Thomas J. Stanley

Secrets of Six-Figure Women–Barbara Stanny

Smart Women Finish Rich–David Bach

Rules of Money–Ric Edelman

Ric Edelman also has a radio show worth listening to[16].

Kiplingers[17] has a wealth of information and great newsletters. You can find them online.

While these titles may suggest the books are all about becoming rich and wealthy, they are full of solid financial wisdom.

It is equally important to define what is important about money to you. By asking this question and digging deep for answers, you will be better able to evaluate what you want out of life and what you are looking for. And therein lies the foundation for your financial plan. Remember, money is not the end-all, be-all. It is simply a tool that helps you reach your specific goals. It is a tool that can bless your family and others and advance the kingdom of God.

While it may seem surprising, the Bible talks about money, wealth, and possessions hundreds of times. This is perhaps because money is a heart issue. How we think about money impacts how we behave with it. Do we hoard? Do we overspend? Do we give? Do we do good with it?

The saying, "If you fail to plan, you plan to fail," is spot on. Don't leave it up to chance. Get equipped. Soak up knowledge. Plan your future.

Chapter 3

Control the Chaos

"With organization comes empowerment." — Lynda Peterson

There is a time for everything, and now is the time to act. Time to roll up your sleeves and get busy. You may be wondering, "But where do I start?"

There are two pieces of information that are important to identify. They are: 1) where you are now; and 2) where you want to finish. Both are critical to know before you create a plan.

Imagine planning a vacation without knowing your departure city, date, or destination! No one does that. People plan vacations, weddings, and pregnancies, yet financial planning gets left to chance.

American tennis great Arthur Ashe said, "Start where you are. Use what you have. Do what you can[18]." In unpacking this incredibly powerful statement, the common theme is to focus on taking action. Notice the verbs in Ashe's statement. Start. Use. Do. Our starting point may not be the launching pad we desire. The conditions may not be favorable in any way. Start anyway, even if more tools, skills, or knowledge are needed. Use what you have and DO. Take massive action.

There's an old saying that says, "You can't turn the Queen Mary around if she's tied up at the dock," meaning, get started. Start off and if you need to pivot, tweak, or adjust...do so. But first, you must start.

Where are you now?

In getting started, the first piece of information that needs to be uncovered is to find your money. If you don't know exactly how much money comes in and where it goes once it comes in, it is impossible to build a new financial future. So, go find your money.

Getting started, you are going to:

- Get organized!
- Determine exactly what comes in each month
- Identify all your assets
- Zero in on all your debts
- Pinpoint all your other financial obligations

That can sound like a chore that's easier to put off. It might even seem a bit overwhelming. I will show you how to do it and then how to stay on top of it going forward. Remember the acronym KISS? Well, we are going to keep it simple, silly. So, don't quit before getting started!

My friends say I am a little bit of an organized freak, and they are right. I'm that person whose closet is color-coordinated, from white to black. Everything has a home, and anyone can easily find something in my refrigerator or pantry. My spice rack is alphabetized. I want my towels folded a certain way. I like my books on the shelf in a particular manner. My garage, my tools, my yard stuff–all organized. My seasonal decor is in plastic tubs that are the color that identifies the holiday. When I had a CD collection, it was alphabetized. I'm that crazy girl. I believe everything has a home, and that is where it belongs! It used to drive my kids crazy until they grew up and adopted some similar habits.

Now, my kids have a similar order in some aspects of their life and home (See, kids really do pay attention!). Being organized will help you stay on top of your finances and better understand where you are and where you're heading. It removes chaos, which frees up your mental bandwidth–and that feels fantastic.

Paperwork is the same way, especially important paperwork. But I also like to keep things simple. Otherwise, I hang onto too much and accidentally toss things I should have kept. So here is my suggestion. Get a 3-inch notebook and a package of dividers, or create a folder and subfolders on your computer. All your important stuff is going in this area. No more sifting through a file drawer. For those who do everything on a mobile device, I strongly encourage you to create an electronic file of all your important papers on a laptop or tablet.

Here's how to label your notebook tabs and/or electronic file folders:

- Marital Settlement Agreement
- Income
- Checking Accounts
- Savings Accounts
- Retirement (401K, IRA)
- Investment Accounts
- Life Insurance
- Tax Returns – (7 folders for 7 yrs. returns)
- Rent / Mortgage Accounts

- Household Accounts (utilities)
- Loans / Other Liability Accounts
- Credit Card Accounts
- Home Warranty

I promise once you do this first task, you will feel more organized and a sense of peace and control coming into place over your financial world.

Gather Your Stuff

Now that you have your tabs or folders set up, the next thing to do is take an inventory of what you have. To do that, you must gather your "stuff."

We will start with income documents. Gather your income statements. If you keep paper copies of your check stubs, go ahead, and collect those. If not, log into your online payroll system and, at the very least, print out your most recent Year End pay stub and your most current pay stub. If you have irregular income such as commission income, overtime, bonuses, etc., I highly recommend printing out each paystub for the past several months.

Now, put together all your expenses. Gather your statements of everything you pay each month, quarterly, and annually. This includes your mortgage or rent, insurance, HOA, all your credit card statements, student loan payments, car payments, boat payments, cell phone, cable, internet, energy, water bill, pet bill, babysitter, kids' sports & activities, gym membership...get it all together. If you don't have paper statements for everything, download your last statement.

And, of course, don't forget the marital settlement agreement. It is so important to keep this document in a safe place. When obtaining home financing as well as meeting with a financial advisor, this document is of utmost importance.

Once you have all the above documents, sort them into the appropriate categories and place them in the notebook or electronic folders.

Income – in this folder, place all your payroll check stubs, any stubs, or statements for 1099 income or odd jobs. If you receive child support, alimony, foster income, social security income, pension income, retirement income, and disability income, keep those documents here as well. Also, keep any reimbursed expense payments here.

Side Note: if you receive social security benefits, pension benefits, or any other similar income, be sure to keep the annual award letter sent to you, which spells out the exact benefit for the coming year. You never know when you may be asked to provide this document, and it is important you keep it handy.

Checking Accounts – If you have multiple checking accounts, you may want to create separate folders for each account. Keep your monthly bank statements and notices here. If you are paperless, download your statements to an electronic folder. Most institutions keep 6 to 12 months of statements easily accessible online. Once they fade away into the archives, they are a little tougher to get your hands on.

Savings Accounts – If you have more than one savings account, you may want to create separate folders for each account. Keep your monthly bank statements and notices here. You may also want to keep any 529 plan statements here as well since those are college savings plans.

Retirement (401K, IRA) – This is where you will keep all your retirement account statements. If you have more than one, you may want to keep them in separate folders. Store your quarterly statements in this folder. Keep or print out from your online account your investment options and performance. These are helpful to have handy, and you may want or need to refer to them often.

Investment Accounts – Just like your retirement account folder, you will want to file your quarterly statements in this folder. Use this folder for any investment account that is not a retirement account. That may be a money market account, mutual funds, stocks, bonds, etc.

Life Insurance – In this folder, place a copy of your life insurance policy as well as any statements pertaining to your term life, whole life, or universal life policies. If you have an umbrella policy, which I recommend having, include this as well.

Tax Returns – It is important to keep copies of your tax returns and all documents used in their preparation, such as W2s, 1099s, 1098s, etc. Hopefully, you've saved them. If you haven't, you will want to ask your CPA or tax preparer for a copy. You can also order a transcript from the IRS. Since you are now single, it is important that you have a copy of at least the last two years. You may need these if you are going to buy a home, and they could be difficult to obtain from an ex-spouse later.

Rent/Mortgage Accounts – File your monthly mortgage statements in this folder. If you rent, file a copy of your lease. Keep copies of your paid receipts for online bill payments. You never know when you might need them.

Household Accounts – This category is for anything relating to the home. Keep receipts here for home improvements, smart home features, and major home repairs such as a roof or a new hot water heater. You may not have anything to put in this category yet, but you will at some point.

Loans/Other Liability Accounts – In this folder, keep all your papers for any loan accounts you may have, such as a car lease or purchase, student loans, personal loans, etc. Keep the loan paperwork as well as any statements.

Credit Card Accounts - Retrieve the most recent statement for each credit card in your name. If there are joint accounts assigned to your ex-spouse in the divorce agreement, we will address this in a later chapter.

Home Warranty - You may have obtained a home warranty when you purchased your home. Make sure you have the important steps for filing a claim or requesting service handy.

By putting the statements in notebooks or electronic folders, you are beginning to feel the organization taking place.

Get Organized

With all your documentation collected and organized, it is time to put it all together in a worksheet so you can begin to budget.

The back of this book contains a worksheet for you to use, By The Numbers.

First.... let's explore your income. Retrieve your paystubs from your Income Folder. Look at your most recent paycheck stub.

Using the By the Numbers worksheet at the back of the book, answer the questions and complete the information.

Second, pull out all your credit card statements. Highlight your credit limit, current balance, the monthly payment (the minimum amount required), the due date, and the interest rate. After doing this, complete the credit card section.

Finally, go back to the worksheet and do the same thing with any installment accounts you may have. Your worksheet should now be complete.

Your current financial picture will begin to take shape, which will give a sense of accomplishment and clarity.

By identifying your income and your installment and credit card debt, you have taken the first step in creating your new financial life.

Being organized is the first step to balancing life's financial ups and downs.

"Now that you know these things, you will be blessed if you **do** them" John 13:17. Therein lies the challenge – *if* you do them.

"Whatever you **do**, work at it with all your heart, as working for the Lord, not for human masters, since you know that you will receive an inheritance From the Lord as a reward. It is the Lord Christ you are serving." Colossians 3:23-24

Chapter 4

Own your numbers

Sit down and estimate the cost

One of Jesus' disciples, Luke, asks a very direct question: *"Suppose one of you wants to build a tower. Won't you first sit down and estimate the cost to see if you have enough money to complete it?" Luke 14:28*

We've all been on vacation before. And when we were making our vacation plans, if we were driving, we figured out our route and calculated how long it would take to get there, bathroom stops and all. Or, if flying, we checked out all our options, booked a ticket in advance, and planned for transportation to and from the airport. We request time off from work. Find someone to water the plants, take care of the dog, etc. Think of all the planning that goes into one week of our life.

Yet...how much planning do we do for our financial future? We weren't taught to do this. While it's not really a good excuse, the truth is, we probably didn't know any different. Therefore, most of us haven't planned our financial today, much less our financial tomorrow.

One of the most valuable things we can do for the benefit of our financial wellbeing is to know our numbers, inside and out. And in that knowing, we become the master of the money instead of it mastering us.

Yada is the Hebrew word for "to know." However, it means something a little different than our Americanized translation. It means to know, not just in your head, intellectually, but also in your heart and your spirit.

Just like when we say, "I know that I know, that I know." It's that kind of "knowing." Deep in our spirit. And I want us to yada all our numbers.

Why do I say that? The "financial career girl me" will say: Because if we get them deep down in our spirit, it will be so much easier for us to make decisions. Our heads won't have to convince our emotions when a decision about money comes along. And we won't get into any hot water due to a lack of knowledge.

However, the "real me" will tell you it is much more personal than that. If we know our numbers deep down in our spirit, then we are less likely to live in fear. Fear will paralyze us. Fear will steal our peace and our joy. It will rob us of happiness – and cause many sleepless nights.

Let's make sure fear doesn't rear its lying head. We are going to dig into this and figure out where we are right now. Just like planning the route for that vacation, we need to know where we stand now to build the roadmap to the future.

Here are a few questions to shine the light on our awareness of our finances:

- *Without looking, do you know how much money is in your bank account now, to the nearest $100?*
- *Do you know how much you made last month to the nearest $100?*
- *Do you know how much your monthly bills are, to the nearest $100?*
- *Do you have more than $1,000 in savings?*

And finally, this question is the hardest –

What percentage of your net income did you save last month?

Not dollars, but percentages. Focus on percentages.

My goal is that you'll be able to answer those questions and more by the end of this book!

"If any of you lacks wisdom, you should ask God, who gives generously to all without finding fault, and it will be given to you." James 1:5

In talking with many suddenly single women clients, the common theme I hear is that they feel overwhelmed when it comes to getting their arms around their finances. For many, their husbands took care of most of the decisions and details. Although we all may like to have a "do-over" to do things differently, the good news is it isn't too late to start managing your money.

This is where tough love comes in. We must all take responsibility for our financial well-being. The past needs to be left in the past - no one can change what happened yesterday or what we did or did not do. No need to beat ourselves up. All we can do is begin anew and vow to do things differently. We can't throw a temper tantrum or vent to our friends and family and expect things to take care of ourselves. We must do the work. And later, we can reap the rewards.

Proverbs 10:17 instructs us– *"Whoever heeds discipline shows the way to life, but whoever ignores correction leads others astray."* Discipline is hard. Obedience is hard. But the lack of discipline can destroy us.

Just like faith comes from hearing the Word of the Lord, financial wellbeing comes from wisdom, discipline, and obedience.

Wisdom–the soundness of an action or decision with regard to the application of experience, knowledge, and good judgment.

Discipline–the practice of training people to obey rules or a code of behavior, using punishment to correct disobedience.

Obedient – submissive to the restraint or command of authority; willing to obey

Spending Plan

Once all financial statements are gathered and organized, the next step is to get your arms around the numbers. How much comes in, how much goes out, and where it goes. As a single woman and financially responsible person, knowing who is responsible for what payments is also important.

For the divorcee, the marital settlement agreement[19] spells everything out. This important document spells out who is responsible for what. Don't rely on what someone says or memory. Rely only on the written document. Always. Think of this document as a rule book for the budget and navigating income and expenses.

Most people cringe at the word budget. If that's you, it's okay. As discussed in an earlier chapter, think of this as a spending plan, a blueprint, or a roadmap to your financial well-being. Having a plan is critical to your success. It's no different than joining a gym to get fit. We still must put on our workout clothes, go to the gym, pick up the weights, or hop on the elliptical. The gym can't do it for us. We must take action.

The budget is a plan. And if we follow the plan closely, we will make it to the destination. If we don't plan…just like that saying, "those who fail to plan, plan to fail." I don't want to fail, and I'm sure most everyone feels the same way.

Experts in air navigation have a rule of thumb known as the 1 in 60 rule[20]. It states that for every one degree a plane veers off its course, it misses its target destination by one mile for every 60 miles you fly. This means that the further you travel, the further you are from your destination. For instance, traveling from Los Angeles, CA, to Charlotte,

NC, is 2125 miles. Using the 1 in 60 rule, if off by one degree, then the plane would land somewhere around Gastonia, NC. And there is no airport in Gastonia.

One degree makes a difference. Just like boiling water... at a temperature of 211, the water is really hot, but it won't boil. Raise the temperature to 212, and suddenly, as if by magic, the water begins to boil. It's the same for freezing temperatures. While I really can't tell the difference between 33 degrees and 32 degrees–they are both really cold to me–at 32 degrees, we know that everything freezes.

If one degree of change makes this kind of difference, it's easy to see the value in a plan and in having a destination or outcome.

There are three categories of budgeting we will focus on: income, saving/giving, and expenses. As we begin, it's important to have the marital settlement agreement handy.

Income

Provide for your household

"Anyone who does not provide for their relatives, and especially for their own household, has denied the faith and is worse than an unbeliever." 1Timothy 5:8

This is the time to roll up your sleeves and do a little work to put your finances in order. At the back of this book, there is a Spending Blueprint. You'll want to use that as you work through this chapter. In the years I have been helping people, both in the banking world and in the home finance area, I have discovered that many people don't know their gross and net income. They think they know. They are always able to give an answer. However, once I collect their documentation, it isn't unusual they are off at least a little bit. Either direction. Some people short themselves, and some overshoot.

Mark Twain said it well when he said, “the secret of getting ahead is getting started.”

Take a moment to calculate your income based on the paystubs previously gathered.

Look at the gross income on your paystub. To calculate your annual and monthly income:

Hourly rate of pay x hours per week x 52 (assuming your vacation is paid) = annual income

Biweekly rate of pay x 26 = annual income

Semi-Monthly rate of pay x 24 = annual income

For household management purposes, use your net monthly income. This is the amount after your Federal and State tax deductions, insurance deductions, 401K contributions, and any other recurring deductions.

Following a divorce, you may have other income which flows into your household.

With that said, let’s get started with the marital settlement agreement if there is one (also referred to as a divorce agreement or divorce decree), or if there was no marriage, but children, grab the child support document.

The first task is to identify all the money coming in. While the format of the document may vary from state to state, the components are the same. It will outline the separation of property, such as who gets the house and who gets each car. It will also define the credit obligations of the parties and who will be responsible for each account. And it will define if payments will be made from one party to the other, and if so, spell out the type of payment, amount, and duration.

If you are receiving income, it may come in various forms: child support, alimony, spousal support, or separate maintenance. It may also be in the form of monthly payments or a lump sum. It could have an end date based on the age of the children or another time factor.

Let's address the different ways income is received following a divorce:

Alimony

Alimony is financial support paid to one spouse by the other following legal separation or divorce. Its purpose is to assist the lower-earning spouse in covering expenses and maintaining the same standard of living following divorce. This type of support is most often awarded when one spouse is financially dependent on their partner over a period of time and may need assistance while gaining their financial footing.

Often these payments may be called spousal support, support payments, or maintenance payments.

While there is no real difference in the terminology, it does matter when the income is being considered for mortgage financing. Words matter, labels matter.

Until recently, alimony was taxable income to the spouse receiving the payments. It is no longer taxed.

Alimony does not include child support, noncash property settlements, or payments to maintain marital property.

If possible, do not count on this money as monthly income. Instead, use it to build up your savings, reduce debt, take courses to increase your earning power, or launch a business. Invest it in yourself when possible.

I can't stress the importance of knowing your "end" dates enough. I have a friend who received alimony for seven years. For her, seven years seemed forever away, and she enjoyed living off that income. She didn't have a job and talked of going back to school. She never did. And eventually, the seven years came to an end, and she was in a pickle trying to figure out what to do. Don't let that be you.

Child Support

Child support is usually straightforward. It is support provided for the well-being of the children. Child support is provided in an ongoing, periodic payment by one of the parents, and its sole purpose is for the financial benefit of the child.

Even in situations of joint custody, child support may still be required. Every agreement is different; however, the intent is the same. Child support is intended to be used for the care of the children involved. It is designed to maintain the child's standard of living and ensure their basic needs are covered.

Child support payments typically end when the child turns 18 or completes their last year of high school. Some agreements extend it to include college years.

It is important to know when this support ends so you can budget accordingly.

Child support income doesn't last forever. If you have several children, it will most likely phase out as each child reaches 18 years old. While the income is necessary to help you take care of your children, try living off the amount you will receive once you only have one child in the house. With the rest, set it aside for future college expenses or an occasional family vacation. I can assure you that the expenses for your children will continue after the child support has ended.

In addition, if you are buying a home for you and your children and want your child support income counted in your qualifying, it can only be used if it will continue for another three years following the mortgage date. This is especially important to know if you are keeping the marital home and need to refinance it.

Other sources of income that may come from the settlement agreement could include notes payable, income from retirement or investment accounts, trust income, equitable distribution payments from dividing a business, and rental income.

It is important to identify how much income you have coming in from each category. This is important because each type of income is viewed differently in financing- specifically home financing. And, of course, child support, alimony, notes receivable, and equitable distribution income will have an end date, and you need to plan for that.

Saving/Giving

It is more blessed to give than to receive

"In everything I did, I showed you that by this kind of hard work we must help the weak, remembering the words the Lord Jesus himself said: 'It is more blessed to give than to receive.'" Acts 20:35

Proverbs 3:9 says, *"Honor the LORD with your wealth, with the first fruits of all your crops."*

"On the first day of every week, each one of you should set aside a sum of money in keeping with your income, saving it up, so that when I come, no collections will have to be made." 1 Corinthians 16:2

Your first goal is to get to consistently be working the 10/80/10 equation. Let me explain.

10% of your income is going toward tithes, savings, and other giving

80% of your income is going towards your living–mortgage, car, bills, utilities, insurance, food, etc.

10% of your income is going towards lifestyle–your toys, travels, wants, recreation

And as time goes on, work to increase the percentage that goes to tithe, savings, and other giving.

My desire is to manage my finances so that I give more to others and bring glory to God.

Expenses

In it comes, out it goes...

Living paycheck to paycheck isn't a good lifestyle. You must know what comes in and what goes out and pay attention to your money regularly. Make a date with it and keep that date every week.

The worksheet at the back of the book will serve as your blueprint for managing your money. What comes in, what goes out, what is necessary, what is discretionary, what is spent, what is saved. It records it all.

This may seem like a duplication; however, it is helpful to have a summary of just income and liabilities as well as a detailed list of income and all expenses. This is simply about knowing your numbers.

The Spending Blueprint gives you this bigger picture that is important in managing your money. You can use the previous By the Numbers worksheet to help fill this out. And you'll need to grab some of the documents you organized in the previous chapter.

In the top section, complete the applicable fields that match your paystub. If you have withholdings that do not have a category on this worksheet, then put them in the "other" column.

The next section is for the money that goes out. You'll begin with tithe and savings. It is so important to do these first before other expenses. If you don't tithe or save, this is a good time to consider one or both.

Be sure to reference the divorce agreement for any potential liabilities that you are responsible for and include them in your expense details.

The money out-go is divided into housing, autos, insurance, utilities, debt, household expenditures, medical, discretionary, and business expenses. You may or may not have expenses in all these categories.

You may want to have a miscellaneous "other" as a catch-all for those unexpected things that can happen during a month. Ideally, when using this blueprint, you will have the bottom total come to zero. Yep, zero!

Final Thoughts

Your Home

Whether you own your home or rent, housing is typically the largest expense. When my husband and I were separating, we had what I often refer to as the big house. It was a beautiful white brick antebellum home. It reminded me of my home state of Georgia. Since he was asking for a divorce, he was playing nice. He wrote down everything he would let me keep on a legal notepad. The offer was to sell the big house, and I could have all the net equity to buy a home. We also had a home in Cabo San Lucas, Mexico, and a small rental property in Georgia. He was going to keep both of those.

So, we sold the big house, and just as we agreed, I went and bought another home with the proceeds. We weren't divorced. We had not filed any paperwork. All I had was that yellow legal pad with his handwritten offer. He moved to Cabo, Mexico, and I remained in Dallas in my new home. He returned nearly three years later, and we started the divorce process. But this time, it started with me. I was ready to go through with what he had initiated. He didn't like that. He had grown comfortable with our arrangement.

The divorce became nasty, and we ended up in court, where a judge had the final say on property division. He got my house, the Cabo house, and the Georgia house. He got it all. I share this with you as a caution. If you go buy real property (aka a home) in your name only while you are still married, it is likely to be considered marital property. Be careful!

For mostly emotional reasons, women typically want to keep the home. Whether it is because of stability for the kids, the school district, memories, or perhaps even pride, we want the house. In life, both males and females make decisions emotionally, and we justify them with logic. And usually, keeping the home is an emotional decision, and it is often not the best.

I have a friend who fought tooth and nail to keep her home because she had designed and decorated it. She loved that home. It was her project, her baby, her pride, and joy. And understandably so. She ended up winning the home. The sad part was she could not afford the home.

When she finally resolved herself to that truth and tried to sell it, it took forever.

Keeping the home must be a good financial decision. And if it isn't then, we must learn to let go and move on.

Other Debt

If debt has been awarded to the ex, it is important to understand that you are not off the hook. Just because the court-ordered one party to pay does not mean the creditor is letting the other person off the hook. In order to be off the hook, the debt must be refinanced–that goes for homes, autos, credit cards–any and everything.

If you are concerned about your income, or future income, meditate on God's word and what He has to say about that...

God will supply all your needs.

"And my God will meet all your needs according to the riches of his glory in Christ Jesus." Philippians 4:19

Open your mouth wide, and I will fill it.

"I am the Lord Your God, who brought you up out of the land of Egypt. Open your mouth wide, and I will fill it." Psalms 81:10

God clothes the grass of the field. How much more will he clothe you?

"If that is how God clothes the grass of the field, which is here today, and tomorrow is thrown into the fire, how much more will he clothe you—you of little faith!" Luke 12:28

Chapter 5

Take Authority Over Your Debt

"It takes as much imagination to create debt as to create income."

- Leonard Orr

We have all bought things that we had no business buying. Spent money on things with no value. Charged it. Paid on it for months. And sometimes even regretted it. Usually, we don't even know what we have spent or how much has accumulated. It's easier to not look at the statements to see how bad the damage is. Or how it has affected our credit.

Good Debt / Bad Debt

There are two classes of debt. Good debt and bad debt. The simplest way to explain the difference is this: good debt has the potential to increase your net worth or enhance your life in some way; bad debt involves borrowing money at high-interest rates to purchase either rapidly depreciating goods or for personal consumption (like eating out and paying with a credit card).

"Good debt is a powerful tool, but bad debt can kill you." Robert Kiyosaki

Beware. It is defined differently in businesses that extend credit. Good debt and bad debt take on totally different definitions. For instance, good debt may be viewed as debt extended that is repaid on time, so it is referred to as good. Bad debt goes unpaid or is paid late, making it bad.

Why is any of this important to you? Because good debt can help you achieve goals and grow your net worth. Bad debt is very expensive and can derail your goals, your net worth, and even your day-to-day lifestyle.

Let's look at some examples of both.

Good debt includes a mortgage, student loans, and business loans. A home increases a homeowner's net worth 40 times more than that of a renter. Student loans increase your value in the marketplace and your ability to get jobs that otherwise would be out of reach. And business loans help expand the business, productivity, employment opportunity, and eventually net profit. Each of these has a net tangible benefit.

Expensive, bad debts are those that weigh heavily on your financial situation. Credit cards and payday loans fall into this category. Bad debt is debt that enhances or increases consumption. Bad debt is expensive. The monthly payments barely reduce the principal, thus taking forever to pay off.

Another way to look at bad debt is that it sacrifices your future for current desires. Once you are months or even years into paying for it, you might regret those choices.

The bottom line is this: be very cautious when taking out "bad" debt. Keep credit cards to a minimum and use them sparingly.

"For the Lord, your God will bless you as he has promised, and you will lend to many nations but will borrow from none. You will rule over many nations, but none will rule over you." Deuteronomy 15:6

Debt and Your Credit

Debt and your credit rating have a symbiotic relationship. The more debt you owe, the more it weighs on your credit score, which means the higher your usage of credit cards, the lower your credit score. Even if you pay on time perfectly. Even if you pay more than the minimum payment each month.

It is important to pay attention to your credit always. You never know when something might be misreported. And it's important to monitor to protect your information. Following a divorce, paying attention to your credit report is very important, especially if there are any joint accounts.

So many times, clients tell me, "But that account isn't mine anymore. He/she is supposed to make the payments," when we discover a derogatory payment on an account. Just because your ex-spouse was awarded and required to pay the joint Visa account (for example), the creditor did not release you from liability. It doesn't matter what the judge said. You are still legally liable. This means if the ex-spouse does not make the payments, the late payment will show up on your credit report and have a negative impact on your credit score. Not only that, but you will also never know until you obtain a copy of your credit report unless you are monitoring your credit.

And, if that does happen, there's nothing you can do about it. If the payment was late on a joint account that your ex is supposed to pay, you would pay the penalty of the blemish on your credit report. Even worse, if the debt doesn't get paid, the creditor can come to you for repayment. It doesn't matter what the divorce decree states. Even though the ex spouse would be in contempt, it would be very difficult to get the courts to force payment. In the meantime, the creditor will pursue all avenues for repayment, including coming to you.

My recommendation to all my clients is to make sure any joint accounts are closed and the balances transferred to a new, individual account in the responsible party's name as quickly as possible. This is the only way to be protected. This includes credit cards, auto loans, personal loans, and mortgages. Any joint account should be closed.

For this reason, I highly recommend credit monitoring. The only provider that I am confident in recommending is www.myFico.com[23].

Credit impacts many areas of our lives, and it is one of the biggest misunderstood areas of money and finance. Credit scores impact our interest rates for mortgages, auto loans, and credit cards. It also is a major factor in our insurance rates–both home and auto. It affects whether we pay deposits when setting up new utilities. And even cellular providers are checking your score and making decisions based on your credit profile.

And let's not forget employers. Employers check credit now–it used to be limited to the financial services field, but now most major employers will obtain a credit report.

When you understand how credit works and how habits and behavior impact your credit, you have a much better chance of avoiding any roadblocks on the path to your financial future.

Take Aim at your Debt

If you find you are saddled with debt following your divorce, then it's time to take aim and eliminate it.

Many people feel stuck in their debt, like quicksand. Coming off of a divorce, there are a lot of expenses that aren't ordinary. Attorney fees, financial planning fees, CPA fees, etc. Not to mention if you need to move, pay some things dictated in the agreement, etc. The path of least resistance is to just make that minimum monthly payment and "next month" take a deeper look, figure it out, get a game plan, and so on. The challenge is that "next month" we say the same thing again.

Sometimes, we need to get mad at debt (not at ourselves, just at the debt) to pivot and make necessary changes. To fight a good fight...you need to draw on emotion. So go ahead, get mad at your debt. If you are sick and tired of being sick and tired...then getting mad at your debt shouldn't be too difficult.

When I think of debt, I am often reminded of the scripture verse John 10:10, "the thief comes only to steal, kill, and destroy." We can easily insert the word "debt" for "thief." Debt is the thief that steals opportunities, kills dreams, and destroys the future. Debt puts you in the position of living paycheck to paycheck if you're lucky enough to make ends meet. Debt robs you of your freedom. Sometimes debt sends you into bankruptcy. Or worse, foreclosure.

Debt often steals your opportunity of being able to give to charity or your church. It prevents you from making memories with family vacations. Debt prevents you from saving for college or retirement. Debt likely caused arguments with your spouse. It puts unnecessary stress on the individual as well as the entire family.

Following a divorce, debt can wreak even more havoc. Managing a household on one income feels different from a dual-income household. Needs change, and sometimes those impact the household budget.

Just how costly is bad debt?

Pull out one of your credit card statements. It doesn't matter which one. Any will work. On the statement, find the monthly finance charge. Now divide that by the minimum monthly payment. Then multiply times 100.

Here's the equation:

Monthly Finance Charge / Minimum Monthly Payment x 100 = Percent of Interest Paid

Let's take a look at a real-life example:

Monthly Finance Charge	$62.98
Minimum Monthly Payment	/ $95.00
	x 100
Percent Interest Paid	66.29%

In this example, the monthly payment is $95.00, and 66% of that amount goes straight to interest each month. That means the principal is only reducing each month by just over $32. Assuming the credit card balance is $3,000, it will take approximately 93 months to pay it off at this rate. That is nearly 8 years!

Naturally, the balance will gradually come down over time, so the payments will decrease. However, most of the payments will continue to have interest.

Aggravating, isn't it? Does this make you mad enough? I sure hope so!

How to repay–snowball ways

You are about to discover a much more strategic and efficient way of paying off debt than most programs suggest.

One popular program suggests paying off your debts, beginning with the smallest balance card. That is the only piece of information you look for – the small balance.

Another program suggests paying off your credit cards, beginning with the highest interest rate card. Again, you are looking at just one piece of the puzzle – the interest rate.

Here's an example of both of those methods in action:

If you take the path of paying the smallest balance method, you will begin with the Mastercard. Here's what that would look like...

CREDITOR	INTEREST RATE	BALANCE
First Community Bank	12%	$5600
Visa	21%	$4375
Mastercard	15%	$2200

Oh, rats...we need the monthly payment information! That is something that is left out of the equation of the small balance method. Actually, there is no "equation" in that method. But here's the missing info...

CREDITOR	INTEREST RATE	BALANCE	PAYMENT
First Community Bank	12%	$5600	$497
Visa	21%	$4375	$230
Mastercard	15%	$1400	$45

Assuming you are unable to beef up the minimum payment to pay extra and all you can do is the $45, then it will take you thirty-one months before that is paid off. And that is not including the interest charges every month. But even if you could bump it up to, say, $100 a month, it's still fourteen months (not including the additional interest charges) before you free up those dollars to apply to the next debt.

I am the type of person that needs some small successes to help me keep going. If I had to wait 31 months before achieving the first goal, I'd probably give up long before that. Thirty-one months is rotten, and even fourteen months doesn't get me excited for just one tiny card to be paid.

Let's try the other method. The interest rate method. The Visa has the highest interest rate. Making the regular payment of $230 will take nineteen months to pay off. Then finally, we will free up $230 to apply to the next piece of debt.

Well, in my opinion, that stinks too. Fourteen months, nineteen months, ugh...isn't there a way to see some results sooner? Is there a better way?

Glad you asked! Yes, yes, yes!

Being the super-smart warrior you are, you have the special strategic weapon in your Debt-Slayer quiver. But first, you need more information. You need the little-known math calculation.

Discover Your Debt Freedom Point

CREDITOR	INTEREST RATE	BALANCE	PAYMENT	DFP
First Community Bank	12%	$5600	$512	11
Visa	21%	$4375	$230	19
Mastercard	15%	$1400	$45	31

Dividing the Balance by the Payment gives us the Debt Freedom Point.

The lowest number on the Debt Freedom Point chart is where you will start. The chart above tells us that you will pay off First Community Bank faster than any other account in just eleven months without paying any extra. Month after month, if you have extra dough, you can apply it to your debt to the lowest DFP account. Always.

In this example, without spending more money per month, we focus our attention on paying off First Community Bank. It will be paid to zero in eleven months. That will free up to $512 monthly.

You may have heard of the snowball method for paying down your debt. This method has you pay off a specified account first. Once that is paid, you take the money you were paying on that credit card account and apply it to the next one on the list. Both paying the smallest balance method and highest interest rate method utilize the snowball practice. The snowball is effective. The snowball is good.

With that $512 free, we would then apply the snowball technique. Next on our DFP list is the Visa account with a debt freedom point of nineteen months. But we've been paying on it the past eleven months as well, so the remaining principal balance is lower. Using the fixed payment in the table above and the interest rate of 21%, the remaining Visa Balance is $2531. We would add the $512 to the $230 we are already paying Visa, creating the snowball effect.

The new payment of $742 would have Visa paid to zero in about four months.

A total of fifteen months has now lapsed. Visa is paid off, and we now have $742 to apply to our $45 on the Mastercard. This brings our snowball payment to a total of $787.

Fifteen months into our debt slaying, the Mastercard balance is now approximately $949. We can pay this off in just over one month.

Omitting the interest charges each month, all debt would be paid off in sixteen and one-half months!

Did you notice I said "all?" All debt would be paid off in sixteen and one-half months versus one small account in thirty-one months using the smallest balance method and nineteen months paying off the highest interest rate card.

The quickest way to create the most cash flow quickly is always, always, always achieved by starting with the lowest Debt Freedom Point number and working your way down the list.

Remember? It would take thirty-one months to pay off the lowest card balance. And it would take nineteen months to free up extra money for the snowball if we went with the highest interest rate debt.

But this is your money, your finances. So...you decide...which is better?

Thirty-one months to get rid of one tiny payment.

Nineteen months to eliminate one high-interest rate card.

OR...sixteen and one-half months to slay it all?

The Debt-Freedom-Point creates the fastest-growing snowball possible.

Whatever you do, eliminate bad debt as quickly as possible. It only makes you poorer. Have a spending plan. Stick to it as much as possible. Use debt only as a tool in acquiring assets that produce.

This is my prayer for you:

"The LORD will open the heavens, the storehouse of his bounty, to send rain on your land in season and to bless all the work of your hands. You will lend to many nations but will borrow from none." Deuteronomy 28:12

Chapter 6

Multiply Your Benefits

Growing your money and building your net worth may seem like a lofty goal as you emerge from the loss of your spouse. In fact, it may be the last thing on your mind.

Yet if you want to be financially free, you must first fall in love with the idea of saving and investing. You must be dedicated to a much better tomorrow instead of being addicted to spending your hard-earned money on things that don't add value to your future self. You must believe it is possible. You must believe in yourself. And you must have the burning desire.

Time is your most important asset when building net worth. The sooner you start, the more time you have for opportunities to present themselves. The more time you have to purchase assets. The more time you have, the more your assets have the opportunity for growth. Yet, no matter the age, it is never too late to start if you haven't yet already.

Net worth is the value of all our assets, such as bank accounts and property, minus our liabilities like mortgages and credit card debt. The result summarizes our economic worth, which is considered the simplest indicator of our financial well-being.

By going through the exercises in this book, you have already examined income and liabilities (expenses), two of the key metrics necessary to calculate present net worth.

It is important to break down the various assets and liabilities. Not only does this identify what is where, but it also helps spotlight any shifts and tweaks that might be helpful. By creating the list of assets and liabilities, you will arrive at your financial net worth.

Assets

Assets are items with monetary value that you own, such as real property, personal property, and funds in your checking, savings account, and retirement accounts. Assets can also include stocks, stock options, bonds, art, jewelry, business receivables (if you are self-employed), and the like. An asset is anything you own that adds financial value.

There are several types of assets. Some assets lose value while others gain value.

- **Cash and cash equivalents:** This is money in your checking account, savings account, certificate of deposit (CD), or another similar type of account.
- **Liquid assets:** Liquid assets are cash or the things that can be sold and converted to cash quickly, like stocks and bonds.
- **Tangible assets:** Tangible assets are physical objects or the assets you can touch. Examples include your home, car, boat, art, and jewelry.
- **Intangible assets:** The nonphysical assets like stocks, bonds, pensions, and royalties
- **Illiquid or fixed assets:** Illiquid assets refer to assets that are not easily converted to cash–they usually take longer to convert, and their value may change in the process. For example, real estate. It may take a while to sell it, and the value could increase or decrease during that time. Other examples are items such as art and antiques. While the word "illiquid" may conjure thoughts of

being something to avoid, don't let that word mislead you. Real estate is one of the best assets a person can hold. It just isn't liquid.

- **Fixed-income assets:** These assets provide a fixed income. An example would be government bonds. Purchasing government bonds is an investment whereby money is lent (in this case, to the government) in exchange for an interest payment. Other forms include certificates of deposit and securities. Fixed-income assets generally don't produce a high return. However, they are generally stable.
- **Equity assets:** This is an ownership interest in a company, like stocks, mutual funds, and retirement accounts.

The value of tangible assets like cars and antiques isn't as clear-cut as cash and cash equivalents; you can't simply log in to an account and check the balance. The original price you paid or the retail price of an item can serve as a benchmark to identify current value. For a car, you can use a Blue Book to obtain value. Other assets such as art and jewelry may need an appraisal by an appraiser that specializes in each asset.

Sometimes the value of an asset is offset by a liability. A perfect example of this is a home. If one owns a home with a market value of $500,000. That would go in the asset column. And if that home had a mortgage against it for $350,000, that mortgage would go into the liability column. The net result of $150,000 is considered equity/net worth.

Liabilities

Liabilities are debts and obligations one owes. There are three categories of liabilities: current, non-current, and contingent. Here's a brief description of each:

Current liabilities are short-term liabilities, which means they are due and payable within one year.

Non-current liabilities are long-term liabilities. They have a duration of more than one year.

Contingent liabilities are often seen in a divorce. Contingent liabilities are debts that a court orders one party to pay, yet it does remove the other party from the legal obligation of paying the creditor. An example of this is a mortgage. If the marital home is not sold until it is refinanced into the awarded party's name, both parties are legally responsible, even if the judge requires one party to pay the full payment monthly.

Liabilities include mortgages, auto loans, student loans, credit card debt, and any other debt.

Net Worth

Both your assets and liabilities come into play when determining your net worth. Your net worth is the amount you own versus the amount you owe. Your net worth will fluctuate; however, it is not the day-to-day value but the overall trend that matters. Following a divorce, net worth is reduced. However, with sound planning, your net worth ideally should grow.

Regardless of your financial situation, now you have a gauge of your net worth which will help you evaluate your current standing and plan for the future. By knowing where you stand financially, you will be more mindful of your spending, better prepared to make sound financial decisions, and more likely to achieve both your short-term and long-term financial goals.

Here's the important thing – you must pay attention to your finances on a regular basis if you want to grow your net worth. It will not happen without your attention.

Start where you are

You may be thinking, "I don't have a net worth nor any money to manage." You may be flat broke right now. Or your debt may be so sky-high you feel there isn't enough money left over to do anything with. I have been there and got the t-shirt.

If you are feeling a bit upside down financially, don't panic. There is always a way to change direction and end the cycle.

1. First, stop spending on luxuries as if they are necessities.
2. Go back to Chapter 4 and create your budget if you didn't already.
3. Save before paying bills. Set up an auto-transfer to your savings and investment account with every paycheck. Even if it is only $20 to start, start and be consistent.
4. As your pay increase, increase your savings rate instead of your luxury purchases.
5. Prioritize your future by maximizing your 401K contributions. And if you don't have a 401K plan, max out IRA contributions each year.
6. Buy assets that pay for your expenses.
7. Don't get caught up spending your future instead of investing in it.

Investments

The Parable About Investment

14-18 "It's also like a man going off on an extended trip. He called his servants together and delegated responsibilities. To one, he gave five thousand dollars, to another two thousand, to a third one thousand, depending on their abilities. Then he left. Right off, the first servant went to work and doubled his master's investment. The second did the same. But the man with the single thousand dug a hole and carefully buried his master's money.

19-21 "After a long absence, the master of those three servants came back and settled up with them. The one given five thousand dollars showed him how he had doubled his investment. His master commended him: 'Good work! You did your job well. From now on, be my partner.'

22-23 "The servant with the two thousand showed how he also had doubled his master's investment. His master commended him: 'Good work! You did your job well. From now on, be my partner.'

24-25 "The servant given one thousand said, 'Master, I know you have high standards and hate careless ways, that you demand the best and make no allowances for error. I was afraid I might disappoint you, so I found a good hiding place and secured your money. Here it is, safe and sound down to the last cent.'

26-27 "The master was furious. 'That's a terrible way to live! It's criminal to live cautiously like that! If you knew I was after the best, why did you do less than the least? The least you could have done would have been to invest the sum with the bankers, where at least I would have gotten a little interest.

28-30 "'Take the thousand and give it to the one who risked the most. And get rid of this "play-it-safe" who won't go out on a limb. Throw him out into utter darkness."

Matthew 25:14-30 Message Bible

401K Retirement Account

No one wants to think of getting old. There are so many anti-aging products on the market - which proves the point. Yet aging is a real thing. And retirement is in everyone's future.

Planning vacations is more popular than planning for our retirement. And that shows up in surveys and studies regarding retirement. Too many Americans are ill-prepared. A study by GoBankingRanks[24] conducted in 2019 showed that 64% of Americans expect to retire with less than $10,000 in their retirement accounts. That is called retiring broke. Just 20% have between $10,000 and $100,000.

If your employer offers a 401(k) plan, check the box "yes" to participate. A 401(k) plan is an employer's retirement savings plan. Each year you elect the percentage of your income you want to contribute. Some employers match your contribution.

Contributions are deducted from your paycheck and invested in funds the employer chooses from available offerings. You can elect pre-tax dollars to be contributed, which lowers your tax withholdings. In this situation, you will pay the taxes due when the money is distributed during the retirement years.

You can also elect your contribution with post-tax dollars. This is called a Roth 401(k). You are not taxed at withdrawal since you pay taxes on the money before it goes into the fund.

There are pros and cons to each and should be reviewed with your financial planner.

Whichever route you take, take one. Take advantage of your employer offering a 401(k) and begin saving for your retirement.

In addition, be sure to play around with a retirement calculator to determine how much money you will want and need in retirement. You don't want to underestimate.

IRA's

If your employer does not offer a 401(k), or if you are self-employed, start contributing to an IRA. An IRA is an Individual Retirement Account. Just like 401(k)s, you can contribute with pre-tax and post-tax dollars. IRAs have contribution limits, with a "catch-up" amount for people over 50. Money can be withdrawn at age 59 ½ without incurring a penalty. At age 70, the IRS requires you to take Required Minimum Distributions (RMDs).

Market Investments

In the world of investments, there are many types of risk as well as varying degrees of risk. While it is different for each investment vehicle, they all manifest in the same way. Risk causes investment values to fluctuate. This fluctuation is usually referred to as volatility. Think of it as a roller-coaster ride. And the premise is that all investments are volatile–there is no such thing as a risk-free investment.

Work with a professional financial advisor who will equip you to make educated decisions about where to place your money. Common investment vehicles are stocks, bonds, options, futures, mutual funds, annuities, digital currencies, EFTs, etc.

Here are a few simple questions that Doug Andrew recommends asking when making decisions about where to put your money:

- Is it liquid? Can you get your money when you need to get it?
- Is it safe?–is the principal safe so that no matter what happens in the economy, you will not lose your principal?

- What is the rate of return? Does it have a rate of return equal to or better than the cost of inflation?

Real Estate

Real estate is a great way to build your net worth and generational wealth. Wealth grows through compounding, which we previously discussed. Historically, real estate has consistently compounded. According to data from the Federal Reserve, a homeowner's net worth is 40 times greater than a renter's[25].

Home prices have increased at a national level by 157% since January 2000, using inflation-adjusted prices. In January 2000, the median-priced home was $131,636. Adjusted for inflation, the price is $208,806. In May 2021, the figure is $329,522[26].

We all must live somewhere, and it costs money to put a roof over our heads. Why not own that roof? And have an investment that will increase over time!

Becoming a landlord has its benefits – and headaches. It is an active and time-consuming form of real estate investing. There are many criteria to consider to find a rental that will generate positive cash flow and a return on investment. If you are thinking of dipping your toe into this, here are the main benefits of owning rentals:

1. Amortization (this means someone else pays the mortgage balance down for you each and every month)

2. Cash flow (after all expenses for the property, the amount of net income you make owning rentals)

3. Depreciation (this is the amazing tax benefit that typically makes the cash flow nearly tax free)

4. Appreciation (real estate values rise historically, and this appreciation adds an extra bonus to the benefits of owning real estate)
5. Rents rise with inflation (as the cost-of-living increases, so will the rents you collect)

Remember – those are the benefits. There is a flip side to that as well. It is not as easy or simple as it sounds. Do your research. Find others who are successfully buying and holding and pick their brains.

Flipping houses has been a trend. Flipping means you buy low and sell high. Usually, the home is in rough shape and needs some TLC or renovation to bring it in line with comparable homes on the market.

House flipping is for those who have the stomach for dealing with the rehab process and can adapt easily when a home doesn't sell quickly.

Anyone can invest in real estate in one form or another – directly or indirectly. Here are some alternatives to owning and managing a property:

- Private Equity Funds
- Qualified Opportunity Zone
- REIT (Real Estate Investment Trust)
- Invest in a Syndicate
- Participate in a mini-IPO
- Invest in a Private Debt Fund

As you can see, there are many ways to invest in real estate. And investing in real estate can be an excellent way to grow your net worth.

Of course, all investing depends on your risk tolerance and your short and long-term goals.

If you are looking to build something for your future or if you want to use your money to make more money for yourself, real estate is historically a sound investment.

There are many differences between investing in the market and investing in real estate. Investing in real estate typically helps produce income now, which could eventually replace your earned income and help you reach financial freedom much sooner.

It can be confusing and overwhelming. But it all starts with making a decision and taking the initiative to start learning. Learn from a professional investing in real estate who will share the good and the bad with you.

Millionaire Status

While becoming a millionaire isn't the topic of this book, there is no reason to think small. Here is an excerpt of an interesting article that appears in Business Insider[27].

Chris Hogan, author of "Everyday Millionaires: How Ordinary People Built Extraordinary Wealth – and How You Can too" has some interesting information about wealthy people and building wealth.

According to a study he conducted, around 33% of millionaires never earned more than $100,000 as a household in a single working year, and only 31% averaged $100,000 a year.

That alone sheds a bright light on the notion that you don't need to make a huge 6 or 7 figure income to become a millionaire. What is important is where those dollars go once you earn them.

"Salary is a factor in building wealth, but it isn't the biggest factor," he wrote. "Millionaires know that how much you make isn't nearly as important as what you do with it."

No matter your salary, what you should be doing with your paycheck is saving at least 20% of it — and living well below your means.

The majority of millionaires in his study hit seven figures thanks to their employer-sponsored retirement plans.

Many millionaires also use a simple investing strategy that's low in risk, according to a self-made millionaire who spent three years interviewing other millionaires: Investing in low-cost index funds.

Set Your Kids Up for Success

A 529 plan is a great vehicle to set money aside for your children's college. This plan is an investment account that offers tax benefits when the money is used for qualified educational expenses, which include K-12, college, and even student loan repayment.

Another idea of setting your children up comes from an article published in MarketWatch in 2019[28].

A strategy is given for setting up your child to become a millionaire simply by saving $1 a day–$365 per year for their first 18 years of life. Each year, that money is invested. In the article, the investment scenario is small-cap value stocks earning 12% a year. With the compounding, the annual investments would grow to be worth $20,348 by the time the child is 18.

When the child turns 18, you stop the contributions and let the money sit and earn a return. From ages 19 through 23, the child funds a Roth IRA with $5,500 each year from her parents' investment account.

Leave it there. Watch it grow. Assuming the growth rate remains 12%, her account is worth $4,185,342 at age 66

If the returns were a reduced 10%, the account value would be $1,455.159 by the age of 66.

Of course, this is just an illustration of compounding and the time value of money. No one can guarantee the results published in this imaginary story, but it would be fun to test it out. And it is certainly an easy way to give your child a head start on saving, investing, and building net worth. You can read all the details on Marketwatch.com

While most people didn't have parents that tried this strategy, I sure wish mine did, and for many, it's not too late to get started.

This is surely a great concept to teach kids and grandkids and get them on the path to generational wealth.

Trusted with Much

"Whoever can be trusted with very little can also be trusted with much." Luke 16:10

I don't know about you, but I want to be trusted with much! We see this in many stories in the bible. For instance, the story of the talents tells the story of the master giving the responsibility of talents to three of his servants. And upon his return, one has multiplied the talents, another has doubled, and the third one was so afraid, he buried them to avoid any investment loss. As a result, the master did not trust the third servant again.

It isn't just money. Our Father is faithful, and he always honors his promises. Our job is to be good stewards of money, gifts, talents, time, knowledge, and so on.

If we back up just a little bit in Luke 12:48, we discover, "from the one who has been entrusted much, much more will be asked."

If you have heard that line of wisdom, you know it means we are held responsible for what we have. If we have been blessed with talents, wealth, knowledge, time, and the like, it is expected that we benefit others.

Where our attention goes, our money flows.
The art is not in making money, but in keeping it."
~ Ancient Proverb[29]

Think back to the parable of investing earlier in this chapter. The first two servants doubled their master's money because they chose to invest it. I find it interesting that the third servant is told that hiding the money to keep it secure was told "that is a terrible way to live!" and he went on to say that living cautiously like that is "criminal."

Which one are you, the first, second, or third person?

If you have been "playing it safe," maybe it's time to go out on a limb and put your money to work for you. Of course, by all means, seek wise counsel when doing so!

It takes time to create wealth. It takes time for money to grow. The sooner you start, the more you'll have.

Chapter 7

Put On Your Armor

"Finance is not merely about making money. It's about achieving our deep goals and protecting the fruits of our labor. It's about stewardship and, therefore, about achieving the good society." – Robert J. Shiller[30]

No matter what stage of life you are in and the activities you participate in, it is important to make sure you have protection. There are so many options available that it could take up this entire book. Rather than do that, I want to outline a few areas to give your attention to. However, this is not insurance advice, and I'm not suggesting you limit yourself to just these mentioned below. I highly recommend choosing an insurance professional and discussing your needs, desires, and concerns. The insurance advisor can guide you based on your needs.

What I share here is simply to open your mind and make you aware of some of the many options in the marketplace.

The main point here is to protect yourself.

Protect Your Identity

Speaking of protection, the first line of defense is protecting your identity.

For a married couple, financial identity has likely been comingled. With joint checking accounts, credit cards, and mortgages, each person has access to personal information such as social security numbers.

While it may seem surprising, identity theft in a divorce is not uncommon. Especially if the majority of credit was obtained in one spouse's name and the other spouse is struggling to rent or obtain utilities and other credit in their name.

There are a couple of things that can be done for protection.

First, freeze credit files. By placing a credit freeze on your report, no one can obtain a report without requesting you lift the freeze. This puts the power in your hands to restrict access to your credit report.

Secondly, monitor credit regularly. A monitoring service sends notifications every time you change your credit profile. The site www.annualcreditreport.com[31] is a consumer site that allows consumers to access their free annual credit report. For monitoring, I recommend www.myFICO.com. However, it is not free.

While you may not have any concerns about a former spouse using your information, it may still be beneficial to take precautions to protect your credit. Cleaning up credit after identity theft can take years and may not ever be resolved in some situations.

Even if you have bad credit or no credit, it is still important to protect your identity. It takes time to improve bad credit or build brand new credit. Don't open yourself up to having a scammer steal your progress.

Marital Accounts

Many divorcing couples have joint credit accounts, whether installment loans or revolving credit cards. And the divorce agreement always states who will be responsible for the repayment of those trade lines.

Here's where there is little understanding... just because the Judge or the court says one person is responsible for paying the obligation does not mean the creditor views it the same way!

The creditor has a legal contract with the borrowers. That contract is binding. If both parties are on the account, both parties are contractually responsible.

Let's take a look at Bob and Sue:

Bob and Sue's divorce agreement states that Bob is responsible for his auto loan payments as well as the joint Mastercard and joint Lowe's card. Bob moves out of the marital home, so he changes the address on the accounts. Months after the divorce, Bob's income is reduced, and things get tough. Sue has no clue. Bob gets slower and slower paying the bills. Eventually, he is 30 days late. Then he can't catch up. Every month he falls behind.

Sue doesn't know because the creditor is notifying the address on the account. Several months go by. Sue needs to trade in her car, so she goes to trade it in for something new. When the dealership pulls her credit, they notify her she has multiple delinquencies on her credit, and her score has dropped. This is going to cost her.

Sue argues that those credit accounts are no longer hers. But they are.

The only way to remove someone from a credit obligation is to open a new account, transfer the balance and close the joint account.

Mortgage Accounts

The only exception is possibly the mortgage. The Garn-St. Germain Act[32] of 1982 may be the remedy. The Act's primary purpose was to ease pressures on both banks and savings and loan institutions and intended to combat inflation during a time when inflation had spiked into the double digits. Like most bills, there were other items that slipped in. One was a substantial benefit for real estate owners.

This benefit allows consumers (homeowners) to place the mortgaged real estate in inter-vivos trusts[33] without triggering the due-on-sale clause, allowing banks to foreclose and collect the outstanding balance when ownership of a mortgaged property is transferred.

That may sound like Greek to you. This means that the person keeping the house (the assumptor) obtains an ownership interest in real property from the ex-spouse and accepts all responsibility for the terms, payments, and obligations.

Here's the challenge. When a former spouse assumes ownership and the responsibility of a mortgage, there is no guarantee the mortgage lender will release the original borrower from their financial obligation of the mortgage.

As you might imagine, this takes some work to put into effect. The lender must be contacted via mail with a request to transfer ownership along with a copy of the divorce agreement.

Covering Your Assets

Insurance coverage is something we all need, and we need to know what our policies cover and who to contact in the event we need to utilize our insurance. While this may sound obvious to many, I've had a few clients with teenage drivers become suddenly single. And they did not know who their provider was nor the protection provided for their teens or themselves.

When my girls were teenagers, I was very fortunate their stepdad was familiar and proactive in the ways to protect our family from financial catastrophe. I'll never forget him telling me that we must prepare for the worst. His worst-case scenario was that an accident occurred on our property or as the result of something one of the kids did or did not do.

Typically, his talking points would point out a narrative of teenagers goofing off in the pool and someone diving in the pool, hitting their heads, and suffering a tragic injury. As he would walk through this imaginary story, it would result in the teenager needing critical care, astronomic hospital bills, and being sued by the other party. And that's just the financial aspect. The thought of a child being seriously injured is grieving beyond words.

For this reason, and many other possible tragedies, we always carried an umbrella policy.

The other imaginary story he would tell was one in which one of our teenage drivers was the cause of a horrific accident, a serious injury occurred (or worse), and we are sued and, as a result, lose everything.

Never did either of us imagine that story in reverse. That the injured party would be my daughter.

My oldest, at age 15, was a passenger in a car with another teenage driver. The driver made an inexperienced decision that led to a multi-car accident. My daughter was ejected from the car and flung across three lanes of traffic into the gutter. She sustained a head injury, was comatose, and had epileptic seizures when paramedics arrived. The paramedics had her care flighted to the trauma hospital. For two days, doctors would not even give us a 50/50 chance of her living. She did live by the grace of God. In fact, God healed her completely. She was in ICU for quite some time before being moved to a step-down unit, then eventually released.

After her release from the hospital, we had months of physical therapy, cognitive therapy, and life-changing activities. While we had good medical insurance, the driver and his family were barely covered. They had $20K accident coverage and auto insurance. That wasn't enough to pay for the care flight trip.

That event was 23 years ago, and it still touches my nerves. While it isn't nearly as raw today as it was then, I still remember the pain. It is a pain that no parent should go through. Yet, it is a pain that refines; it strengthens. Just like the diamond, the pressure is intense beyond words. If you let it shape you, it will make you strong. It will make you tough as nails. And it can make you shine beautifully, just like a diamond.

And here's the thing–we didn't go after the other family. We didn't ask them to pay for anything. All we really cared about was taking care of my daughter and restoring our family. And while we didn't even take a moment to consider suing them, the insurance company did. And that is what happens. The insurance company wants to be whole and expects the "at fault" party to pay up. This is why it is vital to protect your family against all sorts of accidents. I believe there is no such thing as too much insurance.

Bad things do happen to good people. Bad things happen to people who are prepared for bad things. Bad things happen to good people trying to do the right thing. No one is insulated from something bad or tragic.

There are many types of insurance to protect almost everything imaginable:

- Home
- Auto
- Life

- Long Term Care
- Business
- Umbrella

Homeowner's Insurance and Renter Insurance

A standard policy includes the dwelling, other structures, personal property, and liability. It provides coverage costs to repair or replace your home and/or its contents in the event of damage. Homeowner's insurance premiums are based mostly upon the value of the home.

If you are renting, renter's insurance protects the named perils in the policy. Often these include vandalism, theft, water damage, and bodily injuries. It can help with the replacement cost of items damaged.

It is so important to understand what your policy covers. Even if it reads like Greek to you, at least know if you have coverage for major flooding. And what is the definition of flooding? What about hail damage? Wind damage? And depending on which part of the country you may be in, earthquakes and hurricanes?

If you have collectibles, check to see if they are covered. If not, you may want to consider having them added to your policy. This can include art, jewelry, musical instruments, and so forth.

Know what you've got. Ask your agent to explain your policy to you.

Auto Insurance

Auto insurance is one of the most common types of insurance carried. It's so common that it's often taken for granted. Many don't ever read the policy to understand what is covered and the coverage amount.

If you have teenagers, it's vital to identify which parent is covering the teens and what the coverages are. And while you're at it, if your former spouse is covering the kids, make sure you know how to contact the insurance agent in the event there is an accident!

Auto Insurance covers liability, collision, and comprehensive. Here's a quick explanation of each:

Liability Insurance–This type of insurance is required by most state laws. This form of insurance protects you if you are the at-fault party in an accident and goes toward compensating injuries and property damage to the other parties involved.

Collision Coverage–Liability insurance is additional insurance coverage you can purchase to protect yourself. Collision coverage provides money for accident-related damage to your vehicle (regardless of fault).

Comprehensive Coverage–This type of insurance protects you against theft or other non-accident damage to your vehicle. In addition to theft, this could include vandalism, falling/flying objects, or wind damage.

Life Insurance

Oxford defines life insurance as insurance that pays out a sum of money either on the insured's death or after a set period.

The primary purpose is to provide a financial benefit to dependents upon the premature death of an insured person.

There are three main types of life insurance: whole life, universal life, and term life. Within each of these types, there are variations of each. A few years ago, I sat for my life insurance license exam. While preparing for the exam, I think I may have gone cross-eyed, learning all the different ways a policy could vary. It is nearly mind-boggling. But the good news is there are many options available.

Life insurance is a valuable policy to have on oneself. Work with a professional who will listen to your concerns, goals, and situations to create a plan that works for your overall goals.

Long Term Care

It is said that most people's biggest fear is death. Not for me. I know where I am going. My biggest fear is being a burden to my children when I am old. No matter how many great products I purchase, I cannot use cream, serum, injection, or magic potion to prevent aging. If I don't die prematurely (preferably in my sleep), I'm going to get old (and then hopefully, death will be in my sleep!). I may lose my mind to Alzheimer's (I sure hope not), my body may fail me, or I may be riddled with some type of ailment. Regardless of where this path takes me, my greatest desire is to plan in advance to remove the possibility of being a burden to my children.

Long Term Care (LTC) policies provide a solution for daily in-home care, assisted living, nursing home care, and therapeutic care, among other services. Long-term care is generally not covered by medical insurance or a Medicare supplement plan.

Although I obtained my life insurance license, I don't practice, so I will not advise here other than to say - meet with a licensed professional representing a rock-solid company and product to advise you. And for the love, do whatever you can to make all those tough decisions now so your children don't have to later.

The longer you wait to purchase LTC insurance, the more expensive it will be.

Umbrella

An umbrella policy is just what the name implies. It is a personal liability that covers like an umbrella. It covers claims in excess of regular homeowners, auto, and watercraft. Its cover extends beyond the

policyholder to other family members or household members. While it does not protect the property, it does cover injury to others or damage to their possessions.

Umbrella insurance is very inexpensive and worth its weight in gold. If you don't have it already, speak to your insurance agent to see if it makes sense for you to obtain it.

Business Insurance

If you own or operate a small business or are even thinking of starting a business, these next types of insurance may benefit you.

Business: Key Man/Key Person

Also called corporate-owned life insurance (COLI), key man life insurance is purchased by a business to insure the life of one of the company's employees. It's intended to help the company recover from the loss of an employee that contributes significantly to the business if that person's death would reduce productivity or the company's value. An employer might cover the following types of people: top salespeople, executives and other decision-makers, highly visible employees, and employees with unique knowledge or skill sets.

As with any life insurance policy, key man policies have three primary roles:

- **Owner**: The person or entity that purchases the life insurance policy and pays the premiums. The owner has the right to transfer, sell or change the terms of the policy.
- **Insured:** The person upon whose death the policy would pay the death benefit. Therefore, premiums are directly tied to the health and lifestyle of the insured.
- **Beneficiary:** The person or entity that would receive the death benefit should the insured pass away during the period of coverage.

Key man life insurance differs from other life insurance policies in that the business is both the owner and the beneficiary of the policy. The employee essentially has no rights or participation in the policy. However, the business must notify the employee of its intent to purchase coverage on the employee, provide details of the policy, and obtain their written permission before purchasing it. All of this can be done using an Employer Owned Life Insurance Acknowledgement and Consent Form, which can be obtained from the insurer.

Key person insurance is a type of life insurance policy that provides a death benefit to a business if its owner or another significant employee passes away.

Key person insurance may make sense in many circumstances:

- If the business's reputation and financial viability are critically linked to the key employee's name, reputation, or unique skills, the key employee's death could end the business.
- If the death of a key employee (like a top salesperson) could quickly threaten the company financially.

- If a financial institution or other creditor needs collateral for a business loan and requires the option of putting a lien on a key person policy. (This is sometimes called a collateral assignment.)
- If the business is a partnership and each partner wants to buy out the other's shares in case of an untimely death.

A key man policy can also be an employee benefit if the company transfers the life insurance policy to the executive or insured employee. Though key person life insurance premiums aren't tax-deductible, the proceeds of the policy are usually provided to the company free of income tax.

Business Succession

Life insurance can provide needed funding to buy out a deceased owner's share of the business. When a business owner passes away, the continuation of business could be jeopardized when there is no agreement and/or insurance in place. If you own a business, this would be valuable to explore.

One of the most common business succession strategies is the "buy-sell agreement." A buy-sell agreement is one party agreeing to buy the deceased owner's share of the business at a predetermined price from the deceased owner's estate or heirs. This can help ensure the smooth transition of ownership and minimize any potential disruption in business.

Without an agreement and insurance, any remaining owners could be forced to liquidate if the heirs aren't interested in keeping the business and the remaining owners are not able to raise the capital to continue.

When used strategically, life insurance is an incredible tool that can address an array of succession planning concerns.

Chapter 8

Possess Your Land

"My people will live in peaceful dwelling places, in secure homes, in undisturbed places of rest."
-Isaiah 32:18

Home is where the heart is–well, at least that's how the saying goes.

Most people think of their home in emotional ways. It's the place memories are made. Babies are born, kids graduate from high school, and grandkids visit. It's a place to put down roots.

Home can also be any place, any location, anywhere you decide to make it. A place where the people you love are hanging out.

It seems that home is both a noun and a verb. It's a place. It's a feeling. It's inspiration. It's love in action.

A house is different than a home. A house is a noun. It is a place. It's a structure. It's a foundation, walls, a roof, etc. The house is quite likely the largest investment most people make from a financial perspective. It is often the largest asset and the largest liability. And it looks to be, historically, a good path to wealth.

Something often not thought of is that the house is considered the centerpiece of a person's financial picture. For most people, the house has been financed–purchased with a mortgage. This means the bank owns your home, and you as the homeowner have just a small piece of ownership (equity) in the home. Your home really is both an asset and a liability. And it is likely your largest asset and debt.

If you don't yet own a home, keep reading anyway. Learn the value of homeownership.

It is not uncommon for homeowners to have the mindset of paying off the mortgage as fast as possible. Seems smart, right? Not really. But first, let's look at the common methods for that sooner-than-later payoff.

Bi-weekly Method

The bi-weekly payment is making one-half the monthly payment every two weeks, resulting in 26 half-payments, which translates to an extra payment per year. And it seems so much easier on the budget since many of us are paid bi-weekly.

These types of payment plans are often managed via a third-party intermediary. Never forget, everyone is in business to make a profit. The intermediary earns off the "float" generally. They pool the funds and earn interest until the third party makes the mortgage payment.

Doubling Method

There is another way. The doubling method. There is no third party, no automation with this. With this method, the homeowner obtains an amortization schedule that shows the breakdown of each payment's principal and interest portion. Then, each month, the homeowner makes the scheduled monthly payment and applies an extra principal reduction equal to the principal amount of each payment.

In theory, as the principal portion of the payment increases over the years, it is assumed the homeowner's income will also increase. So hopefully, there is no added burden to execute this.

While this certainly will pay off the mortgage sooner, is this the best use of your income?

Target-Year Method

I've seen people do this many times. They determine a future moment when they desire the mortgage to be paid off and calculate from the end date back to the present to determine how much extra principal must be paid each month to hit the mark.

Is this the most cost-effective?

Term-Reduction Method

Many believe this is the smartest way to finance a mortgage–on the shortest term your budget can handle. This results in less interest paid over time and a higher scheduled monthly payment. If the hot water heater bursts or if there is a family emergency, there is no cutting back on this larger payment.

This will certainly enable you to pay off your mortgage faster. But is it the smartest method?

The above methods would help shorten the timeline for paying off the mortgage. Yet each one has disadvantages that most homeowners are not even aware of. Here is what you would give up:

1. Losing control of your home equity
2. Increase the after-tax cost of your home
3. Reduce the return on equity
4. Increase the risk of foreclosure
5. Unnecessarily increase the amount of time to become debt-free

Living debt-free is a beautiful way to live. There is another way to accomplish this.

What if you had assets sufficient to write one big check and pay off your mortgage? Instead of writing a check and paying it off, you pay it off "on paper"–this is as good as paid off.

By paying it off on paper only, you protect yourself against unforeseen financial setbacks such as accidents, illnesses, and natural disasters.

You may be thinking that suggestion doesn't apply to you because you don't have enough assets to write one big check. But there is a way to get there. If you want to prepay your mortgage, it is far more beneficial to take the extra payment portion and put it into a side fund account that will earn a rate of return. The interest income and the compounding effect will put you in a position to pay off the mortgage faster than making the extra payments using any of the methods above.

Plus, having your money in a side account provides you with liquidity, safety, a rate of return, and tax benefits. That is peace of mind.

A home is designed to house people, your loved ones. A financial instrument is designed to house money. Keeping your money separate from the walls of your home is prudent. Allow it to work for you rather than put it into the home where it has no opportunity for growth.

How willing would you be to give the bank some money at zero interest? Let them do what they want with the money. Should you need it later and ask for it back, they charge you interest. That is exactly what is happening with prepaying a mortgage.

Separating the Marital Home

In a divorce, one of the main concerns is the marital home. Who gets it? Do we keep it or sell it? What about the equity division? How do we go about it? These are common questions and should be addressed early in the process.

These questions often take front and center stage, and people tend to forget life must go on after divorce or the loss of a spouse. It is important to explore all the options and ensure you are equipped to follow through before making any decisions.

Valuation

The marital home is likely the largest asset and can be one of the most complicated to divide. There are a few options available to couples. It starts with the question, "sell or keep the home?" And no matter the answer, both selling and keeping the home leads to additional questions and decisions to make.

Before deciding on the "sell or keep" question, you and your spouse must determine the value of the home. Several valuation methods can be used: tax assessed value, real estate agent, or appraiser. Often, the best way to go about this is to obtain an appraiser and request a general appraisal for the purpose of a divorce. This is different than the type of appraisal a lender would conduct for a mortgage.

A divorce appraisal is likely to have a retrospective date of value. This means it is looking back at a previous date, which is usually the date of the marriage separation rather than the current date. It is a general appraisal and written in a different narrative format than that of a market appraisal conducted for the purposes of financing a home.

Some divorcing couples don't always agree on matters (imagine that!), including choosing an appraiser. Sometimes each person obtains their own and then takes the median valuation. It would probably benefit both parties to decide in advance how they will arrive at an "agreed" valuation from dual appraisals.

When selecting an appraiser, make sure they are certified and familiar with your local area. You can use Google to locate them or ask a local mortgage lender for a recommendation. Be sure to read reviews if there are any available. Make sure the appraiser is a residential real estate appraiser, not a commercial appraiser. Appraisers are bound by USPAP requirements and cannot share information about the appraisal with anyone other than his client and the client's attorney unless legally required to do so. This means the information is private unless you share it with others. The appraiser will need access to inspect your home, measure your rooms and property, and provide comparable properties to arrive at a value.

Once the value is determined, reduce it by the amount of your mortgage payoff and any other liens placed on your home. These could be a home equity lien, vendors lien, tax lien, or judgment. If you are not certain of any vendor liens placed on your home, ask your local title company to open a title search. In fact, I highly recommend doing this even if you feel certain there are no unknown encumbrances. It will be needed to sell your home anyway, so better to find out upfront of any items that need to be addressed. The net equity value remains once all liabilities are subtracted, including the cost to sell or refinance.

Equity Division

Whether the house is kept or sold, the division of equity question lingers, "Who gets how much?" And that is assuming anything is left. Most states follow equitable distribution laws. There is no set definition of what is equitable. Equitable Distribution says that property acquired during the marriage belongs to the spouse who earned it. However, in divorce cases, the property will be divided between the spouses in a fair and equitable manner. Since there is no definition of equitable, the court considers various factors.

While many would assume the net equity would be split in half, that is not necessarily true.

Keeping the home

It is not uncommon for many women to fight tooth and nail to keep the home when going through a divorce. For some, keeping the martial home becomes their proverbial purple cow in the divorce. If you aren't familiar with the term purple cow, it is used in marketing to suggest standing out, being unique, and being noticeable. One thing I have discovered over the years in working and speaking with women going through a divorce, aside from the children, it is what women want most. In a divorce, the house, or purple cow, dominates the attention of some divorcing women. And in being so distracted by this aim, their negotiating position is dampened, and often they neglect other areas that deserve equal or greater attention.

The reason women are distracted by the goal of keeping the home is that our brains are wired to seek security. A home represents that for women. Then compound that with the sentimental value–the memories that have been made there. Women see the home as a place to put down roots to raise children and plug into the community. Women are also interested in the investment aspects of homeownership and the pride it provides, but that is secondary to the need for security.

While women have this need for security and get attached to their homes, men seek affirmation and respect, according to brain science. Yes, we are truly wired differently! Men seldom fight to keep the home. They don't have emotional ties, and for them, it's just a house. Notice the word difference? Women usually call it a home, while men often call it a house.

I conducted an anecdotal study of my own by interviewing many of my recent clients after they had been in their homes for six to twelve months. I asked, "How do you feel now that you own a home?" and "How has it impacted your lifestyle?"

The men responded to this question with words and phrases describing pride of ownership and building equity. Women used very colorful imagery to describe their feelings. Women talked about everything from kids painting their rooms their favorite colors, meeting neighbors; the dog having a yard to play in; having a big kitchen to cook in, and having a place for their kids and friends to gather. Women also cited being geographically close to parents or a support system. A few mentioned that they knew it was a good financial decision, but that was at the bottom of their list.

While the reasons may vary, it is very important to address some basic financial questions to make sure keeping the home is a prudent decision and not one that will lead to financial hardship.

Before deciding to keep the home, it is important to count the costs of keeping this home.

Having already determined the net equity, evaluating the cost to maintain the home would be wise before making any decisions to keep it. Here are the things to consider in making a full assessment, which dovetails right into your overall budget:

1. All the monthly recurring expenses associated with the home: mortgage, homeowners' insurance, property taxes, homeowners' association dues, utilities, and upkeep (lawn care, etc.)

2. Major periodic expenses: exterior painting, replacing the fence, replacing the roof, replacing the hot water heater.
3. Periodic Maintenance expenses: replacing air filters, pest control, plumbing, and electrical repair.

And while taking all this into consideration, also remember if a refinance is required to remove the other party or there will be an equity buy-out, there are additional costs. There are costs associated with a refinance transaction, and if the loan amount is increasing due to an equity buy-out, the new mortgage payment will likely be higher than the current mortgage payment.

Many people can keep the home, and it makes good financial sense. And in doing so, it can keep some continuity in the household despite the disruption a divorce creates. However, for some, it is not a wise decision.

Sadly, I've seen many people realize a financial hardship in trying to hold onto the home. Several years ago, a client went through a complicated and high-net-worth divorce. There were assets everywhere. Multiple businesses, several properties, cars, boats, and more bank accounts than I could count. This home held her heartstrings, and the thought of losing it was crushing. Keeping the home had her full attention; it was all she cared about and all she wanted to discuss.

She had dug her heels in, and it was impossible to get her to have an open mind and look at the financial ramifications. Her friends, family, and her financial team tried to help her see other options. If only she looked at other assets (liquid assets), she would see there was enough money to go buy any home she wanted. She didn't want to hear that–it wasn't what she wanted.

She wanted this house–her home–period. And in the end, the court awarded it to her. A year later, she didn't have the funds to pay the property taxes. The upkeep was very expensive, and she could not afford to stay there. She put it on the market during a season that was difficult for sellers. The home sat. The bills piled up. She reduced the price, again and again.

Eventually, she sold the home for considerably less than its value during the divorce. And while waiting for it to sell, the stress she lived with daily took its toll on her body and her spirit.

Equity Buy-Out

An equity buy-out exists when one party is going to retain the home and must "buy out" the other party's interest in the home. Commonly, this is achieved by refinancing the marital home and pulling the equity out in a mortgage refinance.

With the refinance, the home value must support the payoff of the current mortgage, the equity due to the exiting spouse, and any closing costs and escrow payments. If the value does not support all the expenses, the parties need to determine how the shortage is covered.

This is not usually an issue in today's rising home price market. However, if home prices were to reverse course, it would be prudent to map out a game plan...in advance.

The divorce agreement needs to be structured so that the one keeping the home can refinance as a rate/term/equity buy-out. Otherwise, the mortgage would have to be structured as a cash-out refinance, preventing accessing the amount of equity necessary. Another important reason to have financial experts working with your attorney.

When refinancing, the one keeping the home must be able to qualify for the new mortgage. I always urge people to get pre-qualified before committing to keeping the home. This means getting pre-qualified and possibly underwritten before the settlement agreement is finalized.

One of the challenges in qualifying has to do with income. Qualifying income for a mortgage could differ from the borrower's actual income. This is because not all sources of income are considered income under mortgage financing rules. Certain requirements must be met in order to be considered–alimony and child support fall into this category. It is prudent to identify this in advance.

Another area to be mindful of is your credit. It is to your advantage to work together with your ex-spouse to maintain positive histories on joint credit accounts until the accounts are paid and closed. Whether an oversight or intentional, when a mortgage payment is missed, in addition to dropping the credit score, it could possibly derail a refinance altogether. Any late payments on any type of account will hit your credit score and possibly make a refinance difficult, more expensive, or possibly impossible.

Other Buy-Out Options

While the marital home may need to be refinanced, an equity buy-out of the marital home does not necessarily need to be achieved through pulling cash out of the property through a refinance. The spouse seeking to retain the marital home can draw on other separate assets to "buy out" the other spouse's interest in the home. Or can give up their share of other marital assets in lieu of pulling equity out of the home.

An example of shifting assets to avoid pulling cash out might look like this:

The parties have an investment account which is going to be divided evenly. The account value is $200,000, with each party receiving $100,000. The interest in the home, which is $150,000, will also be shared evenly. The wife wishes to keep the home and thus must buy out the spouse to the tune of $75,000. Instead of a cash-out refinance, the wife elects to reduce her distribution of the investment account to $25,000. The husband now will receive $175,000 from the investment account and zero from the home.

In this scenario, the result appears to be the same. But is it? Yes, on the day of the money changing hands, it is equal. However, the future value is probably not. The husband now has $175,000 in liquid cash. He could invest that cash in a manner in which it will grow.

The wife has the house, which has the equity position of $150,000. The home will appreciate over time in most economic environments. However, the equity (cash in the house) will not grow in value. While real estate is a good investment, the cash trapped in the house has no growth opportunities. The wife also has the carrying cost of the home. And, heaven forbid, something catastrophic happens, and the wife needs cash. She will need to pull it out of the house with a cash-out refinance. But if that catastrophic event impacts her ability to earn a living, she may not qualify for the loan, which would prevent her from accessing the money.

Selling the Home

If the decision between the two parties is to sell the home, then the net equity, as determined earlier with the general appraisal, is a moot point. When selling a home, a realtor will analyze homes in the area that have recently sold and come up with a price to list your home. This is likely to be higher than the general appraisal in a rising home price market. It could be the same or lower in a market where homes are losing value. The bottom line is that the home will sell at an amount the market (pool of homebuyers) determines is reasonable and fair.

There are several things to consider when selling the home, such as...

- Who chooses the real estate agent?
- How do we communicate?
- What if we disagree on decisions?
- Who is the point of contact for showings?

Ask and answer these questions early to avoid conflict during the process.

Be Prepared for What you Ask For

Remember the saying, "Be careful what you ask for or wish for?" Well, you just may get it. And it might not be what you want. Or the terms may make you change your mind.

I recall a client who fought to keep the marital home. The court awarded her the home. However, there were some requirements–which are typical. The courts required she refinance it into her name only within 90 days of the agreement. The agreement stated that if she did not refinance it during that period, the court would order the home to be sold and the equity, if any, divided.

Since she had maintained a good nursing job and earned a good living, she didn't even consider that she might not be able to refinance the mortgage and give her ex his share of the equity. But what she didn't realize is she had some ugly blemishes on her credit report. It was going to take time to improve her credit–more than 90 days.

To add insult to injury, the attorney was one who does cheap divorces. As it turns out, my client's cheap divorce became expensive. The decree had to be modified because it did not contain the correct language for the mortgage company to proceed with the refinance and get her ex his portion of the equity (known as "interest" in a divorce settlement). The attorney would not assist, claiming that it could not be modified. She retained a collaborative law firm and was able to get the modification drafted, signed by the ex-husband, and filed in the courts. I remember her breathing a huge sigh of relief.

It took nearly six months from the initial divorce agreement filing to clean everything up and get the refinance handled. In the meantime, the ex-spouse kept threatening to take her back to court and force the sale. All of this could have been avoided with good counsel and an early loan approval prior to the divorce being completed. Anyone considering keeping the marital home would be well advised to get pre-approved for the refinance in advance of the final decree. This allows time to iron out any unforeseen challenges.

Final Thoughts

Don't be intent on keeping the home that you lose focus on your overall financial picture. Your home most likely comes with a price tag. While it will cost you, no matter where you live, make sure you can afford the marital home. Weigh the advantages of keeping it very carefully. Measure it against other assets to ensure you are making a wise decision in setting up your financial future.

Surround yourself with financial professionals who can help you recognize and avoid potential conflicts for a smoother settlement and a successful life after divorce.

References

1. You're Gonna Be Ok, written by Brian & Jenn Jahson, seth Mosley, Jeremy Riddle from the Album After All These Years, release date 27, 2017
2. Blue Letter Bible https://www.blueletterbible.org/kjv/pro/31/25/t_conc_659025
3. Dictionary.com https://www.dictionary.com/browse/strength
4. Dictionary.com https://www.dictionary.com/browse/dignity
5. Bible.com https://www.bible.com/bible/116/ECC.5.19.NLT
6. Ayn Rand https://courses.aynrand.org/works/the-meaning-of-money/#:~:text=%E2%80%9CBut%20money%20is%20only%20a,replace%20you%20as%20the%20driver
7. https://shiftprocessing.com/american-debt/#:~:text=According%20to%20financial%20experts%2C%20the,have%20%2414%20trillion%20in%20debt.
8. https://www.pymnts.com/consumer-finance/2021/new-report-upper-income-americans-live-paycheck-to-paycheck/
9. https://www.statista.com/chart/20323/americans-lack-savings/
10. https://www.gobankingrates.com/retirement/planning/why-americans-will-retire-broke/
11. https://www.gobankingrates.com/retirement/planning/why-americans-will-retire-broke/

12. https://www.bankrate.com/finance/credit-cards/survey-more-than-half-of-americans-lose-sleep-over-money-troubles-2/
13. https://www.forbes.com/advisor/personal-finance/how-to-prevent-overdraft-fees/
14. https://www.goodreads.com/quotes/7374491-do-not-save-what-is-left-after-spending-instead-spend#:~:text=%E2%80%9CDo%20not%20save%20what%20is%20left%20after%20spending%3B%20-instead%20spend,what%20is%20left%20after%20saving.%E2%80%9D
15. https://thecollegeinvestor.com/17145/would-you-rather-have-a-penny-that-doubles-each-day-for-a-month-or-1-million/
16. https://www.investopedia.com/ask/answers/what-is-the-rule-72/
17. https://www.edelmanfinancialengines.com/ric-edelman-radio/
18. https://www.kiplinger.com/
19. https://www.brainyquote.com/quotes/arthur_ashe_371527
20. https://lawlawfirm.com/what-is-a-marital-settlement-agreement/
21. https://en.wikipedia.org/wiki/1_in_60_rule
22. https://bqotd.com/leonard-orr/it-takes-as-much-imagination/
23. Robert Kiyosaki, "The ABCs of Getting Out of Debt"
24. https://www.myfico.com/
25. https://www.yahoo.com/now/survey-finds-42-americans-retire-100701878.html#:~:text=Retirement%20prospects%20seem%20grim%20for,results%20of%20a%20GOBankingRates%20survey.&text=Sixty%2Dfour%20percent%20of%20Americans,-42%25%20reported%20back%20in%20January.

26. https://www.federalreserve.gov/publications/files/scf20.pdf

27. https://dqydj.com/historical-home-prices/

28. https://www.businessinsider.com/how-millionaires-build-wealth-consistency-2019-1

29. https://www.marketwatch.com/story/make-your-kid-rich-for-1-a-day-2014-08-13

30. https://www.proverbsworld.in/2019/10/the-art-is-not-in-making-money-but-in-keeping-it.html

31. https://www.brainyquote.com/quotes/robert_j_shiller_824813#:~:text=Shiller%20Quotes&text=Finance%20is%20not%20merely%20about%20making%20money.,about%20achieving%20the%20good%20society.

32. https://www.annualcreditreport.com/index.action

33. https://www.federalreservehistory.org/essays/garn-st-germain-act

34. https://www2.illinois.gov/rev/questionsandanswers/Pages/526.aspx#:~:text=An%20Inter%20Vivos%20Trust%20is,or%20after%20the%20trustor's%20lifetime.

By the Numbers

INCOME

My income is ☐ hourly ☐ salary ☐ commission ☐ self-employed

My pay periods ☐ weekly ☐ bi-weekly ☐ semi-monthly ☐ monthly

My base gross income per month is ______

My overtime average per month is ______
(take the last 3 months and average)

My commission average per month is ______
(take the last 3 months and average)

My self-employment income is (take home after expenses) ______

My total gross income per month is ______

LIABILITIES

I have ______ (number) credit cards. My spouse has ______ credit cards.

My children have ______ (number) credit cards

Together, the family has ______ (number) credit cards.

List below your credit cards. Start with your highest balance card and work your way down to the smallest balance card. If you need more room, use the additional page.

Credit Card Name	Credit Limit	Balance	Monthly Minimum	Interest Rate
Total / Subtotal	0	0	0	

By the Numbers

Credit Card Name	Credit Limit	Balance	Monthly Minimum	Interest Rate
Page 2 subtotal	0	0	0	
Page 1 subtotal	0	0	0	
Total	0	0	0	

Spending Analysis Blueprint

Gross Monthly Income						
	His Current	Projected	Her Current	Projected	Total Current	Projected
Gross Monthly Income						
Less - FICA taxes						
Medicare Taxes						
Federal Inc Tax						
StateTax (if applicable)						
Other Tax						
Benefit Withholding						
401K Contribution						
Other Withholding						
Net Spendable Income	$0.00	$0.00	$0.00	$0.00	$0.00	$0.00

Monthly Expenses						
	His Current	Projected	Her Current	Projected	Total Current	Projected
HOME						
Mortgage / Rent						
HOA						
Maint & Repairs						
AUTO						
Auto 1						
Auto 2						
Fuel						
Parking/tolls						
INSURANCE						
Homeowner / Renter Ins						
Mortgage Protection						
Auto Insurance						
Life Insurance #1						
Life Insurnace #2						
Other						
Other						
UTILITIES						
Internet						
Electricity						
Garbage						
Water / Sewer						
Telephone						
Cell phone						

DEBT						
CC						
CC						
CC						
CC						
CC						
CC						
CC						
CC						
CC						
CC						
Loan						
Loan						
Loan						
Loan						
SAVINGS						
Savings Account						
Investment Accounts						
MISC						
Household						
Groceries						
Clothes						
Gifts						
Child care						
Medical Expenses/RX						
Other						
Other						
Other						
DISCRETIONARY						
Dining						
Travel						
Entertainment						
Misc						
Education (college)						
BUSINESS EXPENSES						
Cell phone						
Office phone						
eFax						
Office supplies						
Marketing budget						
Other						
Other						
Total Expenses	$0.00	$0.00	$0.00	$0.00	$0.00	$0.00
Total	$0.00	$0.00	$0.00	$0.00	$0.00	$0.00

Made in the USA
Monee, IL
04 November 2026

67381920R00079